W9-CPN-435

PUTTING IMPOTENCE TO BED

Putting Impotence to Bed

What Every Man & Woman
Need to Know

Joseph L. Godat, M.D.

Summit Publishing Group ▪ Arlington, Texas

THE SUMMIT PUBLISHING GROUP
2000 E. Lamar Boulevard, Suite 600
Arlington, Texas 76006

Printed in the United States of America.
03 02 01 00 99   5 4 3 2 1

Library of Congress Cataloging-in-Publication Data
Godat, Joseph L. (Lee), 1930-
   Putting impotence to bed : what every man and woman need to know / by Joseph L. Godat.
   p. cm.
   Includes bibliographical references and index.
   ISBN 1–56530–302–4
   1. Impotence Popular works. 2. Sex Popular works. 3. Sex instruction for the aged Popular works. I. Title.
   RC889 .G626 1999
   616.6'92—dc21
                                                99–6711
                                                CIP

Cover and book design by David Sims
Illustrations by Peter Fan

To Gloria, my inspiration

Contents

Part I

Part II

Part III

THE CAUSES OF MALE IMPOTENCE

Part IV

Part V

Foreword

Robert I. Kramer, M.D.

Professor of Pediatrics
University of Texas Southwestern Medical Center (retired)

Former Chairman
Department of Pediatrics, Baylor University Medical Center

Sexual dysfunction is a topic that has been avoided for many reasons—embarrassment, feelings of inadequacy, fear of losing a partner, concern about being abnormal or different, among others. But with attitudes fueled by repression and ignorance, too many people have prevented themselves from admitting that there is a problem, discussing it with their partner, seeking professional help, or working to resolve their difficulties.

In his informative, rational approach to presenting the facts about sexual dysfunction, Dr. Joseph L. Godat concisely conveys in a logical way the causes, treatments, and cures for this very common problem. As people today are becoming better informed and less apt to hang onto the "skeleton-in-the-closet" attitudes of their parents and grandparents, they should find this book to be an invaluable resource, especially if they acknowledge their problem and are willing to seek help.

Dr. Godat describes female and male sexual anatomy in a direct, scientific, but easily understood manner, which should be of great benefit to the many people who know surprisingly little about their bodies. He addresses hormonal and erotic responses to stimulation, providing clear explanations for the physiological reactions involved. He also offers a most comprehensive list of possible diagnoses for both female and male problems, many of which are directly related to physical causes.

Sexuality has not been part of the education of most physicians, and, as a result, most of them have been either ill equipped or unwilling to approach the subject. The inability of doctors to deal with sex has been compounded in the past by misguided public attitudes that defy logic. In fact, the worthy Kinsey Report and the exhaustive work of Masters and Johnson unfortunately assumed a somewhat pornographic label because of society's inability, at the time, to accept any treatise with sexual content as strictly educational. *Joy of Sex*, despite the best of intentions, was seen by many readers as a "show-and-tell" tome to titillate their sexual fantasies, again because of the sexually repressed attitudes prevalent earlier this century. I believe the information contained here will be received by a much more open-minded public.

Sex therapy, in its formative stages, was much maligned. Therapists were looked upon as being little more than promoters of promiscuity and exponents of kinky sex. Fortunately, we have come a long way in recent decades. Dr. Godat endorses such therapy, stressing the validity of a dedicated organization of practitioners who have no connection at all with previous perceptions. The pleasure he derives from the resolution of a potentially devastating relationship is beautifully conveyed. Equally apparent is the heartache that touches him when he becomes involved with a marriage that is deteriorating because of the sexual dysfunction of one or both partners.

The inability of some women to achieve orgasm is thoughtfully discussed, including reasons for its nonoccurrence and ways to overcome it. Dr. Godat also deftly explains the often subtle and emotional factors that contribute to sexual dysfunction among women and points the way to finally achieving success and gratification. He also explores the perception of men as "macho" creatures, seen as looking on their sexuality in terms of conquests rather than mutually shared intimacies. Now we are finding that men also desire and can benefit from the same emotional supports of love, caring, and passion that for some time have been recognized as necessary to women.

Dr. Godat graphically presents actual case histories where relationships have been saved or even brought to heights of sexual pleasure that never before had existed. Those personal accounts of triumph over daunting sexual difficulties graphically convey what should be seen as the main message of Dr. Godat's book: There is cause for optimism in even the most serious cases, because abundant help is available.

Putting Impotence to Bed is recommended for anyone who has experienced some dysfunction in his or her sexual life. In fact, it has appeal to couples who have no ostensible problems, because the information it contains can make a good situation even better. Dr. Godat has achieved a rare literary combination in that he can be direct and very clinical at one moment and yet be compassionate and very caring at the next. This carefully researched and thoughtfully presented book can be of immense value to the many people whose relationships are fragile because of sexual difficulties.

Preface

The hurt in Sarah's eyes told me far more than her carefully chosen words. And the problem that she said was tearing apart her marriage echoed what I was hearing frequently from other female patients. Sarah's husband had no interest in sex, wouldn't touch her, was subject to fits of anger, and they had been suffering together in silence for some time. Sure signs of impotence, I was beginning to realize.

She had been a patient of mine for more than twenty years, and we had come to share a warm, confidential relationship that I enjoyed and she obviously appreciated. I had delivered her two children, eventually performed a hysterectomy, and I had worried along with her when her husband lost his job and lapsed into a period of heavy drinking and deep depression.

After suffering some difficult times, he finally stopped abusing alcohol, found a good job, and their marriage had seemed to rebound nicely. Now this. Impotence, that unmentionable affliction, was stalking them. But Sarah's willingness to talk openly with me about her situation soon led to help for her husband, eventually a much happier marriage, and a fascinating new area of medicine for me.

One of the great benefits of a long career has been my lasting relationship with patients as they move through the various stages of adulthood—marriage, motherhood, grandchildren, menopause, and the golden years. The truth is, many of us have grown older together. But Sarah's story wouldn't have been told during most of my thirty-seven years of practicing obstetrics and gynecology. Not only were sexual problems in both genders rarely discussed, they also were grossly misunderstood by all of us—doctors and patients alike.

Now a new age is dawning in the treatment of sexual dysfunction, thanks in large part to the current willingness of *women* to talk to *their* doctors about a problem men have been deathly afraid to confront. What I subsequently have learned from my patients and the growing number of victories over impotence that I have witnessed has led me to immerse myself in a study of the problem.

But there have been some interesting twists along my path to understanding impotence. Of increasing curiosity has been the realization that knowledge of female sexual dysfunction lags far behind that of men. So, after originally setting out to explain male impotence to women, I decided my book also should inform women as much as possible about their own sexual difficulties.

Yes, male sexual problems take an immense toll on women, but to ignore the challenge women have with their own minds and bodies would have been unfair. Our determination to examine female sexual dysfunction fortunately coincided with a recent surge in research that is beginning to tell us a lot we didn't know. But we've also learned that female sexuality is much more complicated than that of men, and remains greatly unexplored by comparison.

That said, let's talk about Viagra, the wonder drug that is making millions of men and women feel sexy again. The little blue pill that has taken the world by storm is a major reason why my patients are suddenly willing to discuss impotence with me. The husband who had given up on sex years ago gets his hands on Viagra, and his interest in sexual activity is magically restored. This often leads to physical and emotional problems for his wife, who hasn't had sex for years, and that's where I come in. The trust built up during our longtime partnerships has opened lines of communication on a number of vital health topics with my patients, but none intrigues me more than their recent focus on sexual dysfunction.

My dedication to learning all I possibly can about impotence finally culminated in a project I wouldn't have contemplated just a few years ago—writing a book. But none of this—my ability to inform my patients and you—would have been possible without the contributions of three esteemed colleagues and cherished friends—Connie Engels, an accomplished sex therapist, Dr. George E. Hurt, a noted urologist, and Brenda Garritson, an expert nutritionist. Their support of this project has been invaluable.

There also were two significant sources of information that formed the basis for much of my research, and I recommend them to anyone who wants to gain greater understanding of problems associated with human sexuality. The National Health and Social Life Survey, the first comprehensive assessment of sexual dysfunction in the United States since the Kinsey Reports of fifty years ago, opened my eyes to the shocking prevalence of impotence in our society. An article revealing the findings of the survey was published in the *Journal of the American Medical Association* on February 10, 1999. Also, learning is a constant exercise in medicine, and my knowledge has been significantly expanded by the comprehensive text *Our Sexuality, Sixth Edition*, by Robert Crooks and Karla Baur. It would be an excellent resource for all physicians, educators, and you.

But before you delve into the facts about impotence, allow me to offer some advice on how to proceed. First, I have approached this presentation with a woman's perspective in mind, which makes sense when you consider my specialty. However, I assure you that the partners of the women who inspired me can and should be equal beneficiaries. With that diverse audience in mind, this book has been organized along very flexible lines.

Read the "Impotence Revealed" section first for a solid foundation to support better understanding of what follows—"Women and Impotence," "The Causes of Male Impotence," "Treating Male Impotence," and "A Healthy Lifestyle." Then let your personal needs guide you by going directly to the section that answers your most pressing questions. After that, move about freely among the other parts of the book as well as the subdivisions within them. And don't stop there. Go back and read them again.

Together we can do something about this horrible stigma that has burdened the minds of millions of men and women since time immemorial. Only our ignorance has locked impotence in a closet of shame and misunderstanding for too many generations of sufferers. Now we have available to us the knowledge required for restoring warm intimacy that until now might have seemed irretrievable. After all, sex is a vital component of a healthy, loving relationship, and there is no good reason for any couple to endure the humiliation of impotence and other forms of sexual dysfunction without hope.

Joseph L. Godat, M.D.
July 1999

Acknowledgments

Cindy Brinker, president, Brinker Communications; Jill Bertolet, president and publisher, and Veronica Palmer, vice president of business development, Summit Publishing Group; William Scott, project manager; Mark Murphy, research and development; Charlotte Huff, research; Gwynne Elledge, research; Angie Cantrell, research.

Part I

IMPOTENCE REVEALED

WARNING: SMOKING CAU...ES IMPOTENCE
California Department Of Health Services. © 1999 Califor...artment of Health Services

Workers suspended by a crane place billboard parody of the Marlboro Man smoking a limp cigarette with the word "impotent" alongside, on Sunset Boulevard in the Hollywood section of Los Angeles. The billboard, which replaces a pro-smoking Marlboro Man, is one of 366 tobacco billboards across the state being replaced with new anti-tobacco advertising by the California Department of Health Services. (AP Photo/Rene Macura)

Impotence Revealed

T he Marlboro Man belonged on Sunset Strip, a billboard giant exuding masculinity on a glitzy street in a lusty city. Now, guests at the Chateau Marmont,[1] whose rooms directly faced the plywood icon, warily eye his replacement—*Impotent Man*.

Setting trends is serious business in Los Angeles, which makes the emergence of the cowboy cutout with a flaccid cigarette dangling from his mouth a sobering sign of the times. And while partygoers at the hotel have been known to shoot champagne corks at the new guy bearing the letters I M P O T E N T at his side, many of us are taking seriously his message that "Smoking Causes Impotence."

Running the Marlboro Man out of a town where sex is an obsession— at least on film—was the clever strategy of the California Health Department, thanks to an agreement by tobacco companies to help settle multiple lawsuits by removing their cigarette billboards. Now the spotlight exposes what once was unmentionable not only on the Sunset Strip but also just about everywhere else.

Emerging from the shadows of misinformation, taboos, and repression is a growing realization that sexual dysfunction is a much larger problem than any of us had imagined. The impetus for this awakening has come from two recent breakthroughs that occurred almost simultaneously and triggered a wholesale admission that our sex lives are in trouble.

Half a century after Kinsey revolutionized American attitudes toward sex, a new study by a group of distinguished University of Chicago scholars has revealed the pervasiveness of sexual dysfunction among men and women in our society. And if their findings needed confirmation, it came in the form of an overwhelming response to the pill that has brought sex back to millions of cold bedrooms—Viagra!

The National Health and Social Life Survey didn't produce any shock waves when it was produced in book form in 1994.[2] But when the survey's stunning findings were published in the respected *Journal of the American Medical Association* on February 10, 1999, it gained widespread attention and acclaim. Now we know that nearly half of the nation's women and almost a third of its men are plagued by sexual problems, a rate far beyond what anyone had expected, including the authors of the study. The survey is recognized as by far the most comprehensive look at our sex lives, surpassing Kinsey in breadth and methodology.

A drug called sildenafil citrate also had an inauspicious debut before becoming one of history's best-selling pills. Pfizer Inc. originally tested it as a medication for coronary heart disease, believing the drug's ability as a smooth-muscle relaxer might help relieve severe angina pains. But sildenafil citrate was a washout in that role and was nearly abandoned by the pharmaceutical giant. *Wait a minute!* cried those test patients who also suffered erectile dysfunction. They were ecstatic over the drug's amazing side effect—the best erections of their lives. Welcome to the world, Viagra!

The National Health and Social Life Survey told us that there were as many as 30 million impotent men in the United States, and right on its heels we had a pill that caused a stampede by those who had been suffering silently for years and demanded prescriptions. If there had been any doubts about the NHSLS results, they were erased by the record surge in Viagra sales, which were expected to hit $1.4 billion in 1999 after Food and Drug Administration approval in 1998.

What We Have Learned

■ ABOUT EVERYBODY
■ ABOUT WOMEN
■ ABOUT MEN

As the new millenium approaches, our knowledge of sexuality and what can go wrong has expanded greatly, thanks to a proliferation of research projects and added exposure by the media, all fed by soaring public interest. Here's what we now know that many of us didn't know a few years ago about our sexual problems.

ABOUT EVERYBODY

■ Americans have the most money, eat the best of foods, possess the most sophisticated medical care in the world, but many of them are fat, drink too much, have poor diet habits, take too many drugs, and suffer sexual dysfunction at an alarming rate.

■ Diabetes is the leading cause of impotence, but smoking, illegal drugs, and many prescription and over-the-counter drugs also are to blame.

Cocaine is particularly harmful, constricting blood flow and damaging nerves, possibly on a permanent basis.

■ Alcohol abuse is a threat to the sexual performance of everyone who drinks too much. It impairs the nerves that transmit the message of stimulation from the brain, causes veins to dilate, and leads to vascular "leakage." It is toxic to the testes and contributes to cessation of menstruation and irregular menstrual cycles.

■ Diets high in fat can lead to vascular problems, a common cause of sexual dysfunction. A diet high in sodium and fat contributes to hypertension, which usually is managed by medications that can cause impotence.

■ Lack of exercise leads to people being overweight, which can cause diseases tied directly to impotence. Failure to exercise also weakens the cardiovascular system, which is vital to sexual performance.

■ Broccoli, broccoli sprouts, Brussels sprouts, dark green and orange vegetables, fruits, berries, melons, and soy products such as tofu, fish, and olive oil are all good for your sex life.

■ We are just beginning to understand that good sex is not only about erections and orgasms, it also is about intimacy, closeness, and trust.

ABOUT WOMEN

■ Sexual dysfunction affects 43 percent of the women in this country compared to 31 percent of the men. Also, much more is known about male problems than female difficulties, which are far more complex.

■ Many women never have experienced orgasm, rarely experience orgasm, rarely have multiple orgasms, usually do not reach orgasm through intercourse, and at times fake orgasm. The absence of orgasm during intercourse is *not* a sexual dysfunction.

■ The clitoris is twice as large as described in most anatomy texts, and contains erectile tissue as well as nerves and blood vessels that allow it to swell and engorge with blood during arousal—much the way the penis does in men.

A substance in the body called nitric oxide is crucial to a penis becoming erect. Nitric oxide also is produced in erectile tissue of a woman's reproductive organs, and the same blood-flow problems that cause male impotence affect women, too.

Some physicians already are prescribing Viagra for women, although it is still being tested and is not approved for them by the FDA. And not all wives of longtime impotent men who discover Viagra are pleased. After a long period of sexual inactivity, they face physical and psychological problems with newly turned-on partners.

Recent studies indicate that loss of estrogen is linked to risk of Alzheimer's disease, which is less likely to affect women who take estrogen after menopause.

ABOUT MEN

Viagra works for about 70 percent of the men who take it. Stimulation is required to achieve an erection after taking the pill, which usually takes effect within an hour.

There are physical causes for more than 90 percent of erectile dysfunction among American men. Not long ago most cases of male impotence were thought to be "all in the head."

Smoking causes considerable vascular constriction. The arteries in a penis are incredibly small, so almost any degree of constriction is going to affect blood flow and impede a man's ability to have an erection. Studies show that teenage boys who smoke two packs a day could be impotent before they are thirty.

It's a myth that as men age they will lose their ability to have an erection. As a man grows older, it might take longer to achieve one, but healthy men can continue to attain erections into and beyond their eighties.

Psychological problems are involved in up to 20 percent of all cases of impotence among men. Those symptoms, however, often are a secondary response to a physical problem.

▓ A diagnosis of prostate cancer is not necessarily a death sentence, and it doesn't always mean that surgery is required. But if an operation is necessary, there are new nerve-saving techniques available.

▓ When a man sits on a bicycle seat he is putting his entire body weight on the arteries that supply the penis. Prolonged riding can cause impotence, and cyclists should look into softer seats designed with a hollowed-out area.

The Reality of Our Sexuality

▓ SURVEYING THE SITUATION
▓ DOING SOMETHING ABOUT IT

Bond, James Bond. Sean Connery always will be Bond for most of us, the handsome, virile secret agent who conquered a number of gorgeous women in heart-pounding movie adventures. He's still doing it decades later, although his now grandfatherly appearance wouldn't seem enough to inspire the sexy young females playing opposite him.

Filmdom persists in these winter-summer couplings, but we're now finding out what a mismatch they *really* are. These are the least likely people to do well together sexually despite what you're seeing on the screen. Men of Connery's age group—fifty and more—are three times as likely to report difficulty achieving and maintaining an erection than younger men. That's not so surprising, but those youthful females who are his costars and the focus of our libido-driven media are not the sexpots they seem to be.

They may provide the male world with many of its fantasies, but one of the more striking results of the National Health and Social Life Survey concerns women aged eighteen to twenty-nine. About 26 percent of them said they regularly failed to achieve orgasm, 27 percent said sex brought no real pleasure, and 32 percent said it didn't interest them at all. Also, unmarried women—many of whom are in this age group—were 50 percent more likely than married women to report sexual problems.

There are a number of reasons why so many younger women are miserable in bed, including a tendency to have shorter relationships, longer periods of sexual inactivity, and the fact that they often live more stressful lives. But there is hope for improvement. Unlike men, who face the increased possibility of impotence with age, women as they grow older report fewer problems and more pleasure during sex than when they were younger.

SURVEYING THE SITUATION

Spend some time examining the accompanying chart, which represents the more interesting findings of the NHSLS. The odds are pretty good that you will find yourself represented somewhere among the numbers, and I predict that you will have two reactions: First will be amazement at how thoroughly we have been invaded by sexual dysfunction. Second will be a sense of relief that you are not alone in suffering the problems you might have.

The survey is a sample of 1,410 men and 1,749 women between the ages of eighteen and fifty-nine living in households throughout the United States. The researchers believe the results account for about 97 percent of the population in this age range—approximately 150 million Americans. Each participant was interviewed for an average of ninety minutes, including questions regarding seven impotence-related problem areas:

Respondents' age	Lack interest		Can't achieve orgasm		Erectile dysfunction	Pain during sex	Climax too early
	Women	Men	Women	Men	Men	Women	Men
18 – 29	32%	14%	26%	7%	7%	21%	30%
30 – 39	32	13	28	7	9	15	32
40 – 49	30	15	22	9	11	13	28
50 – 59	27	17	23	9	18	8	31
Marital status							
Now married	29	11	22	7	9	14	30
Never married	35	19	30	8	10	17	29
Divorced, separated, or widowed	34	18	32	9	14	16	32
Education							
No high school	42	19	34	11	13	18	38
High school	33	12	29	7	9	17	35
Some college	30	16	24	8	10	16	26
College	24	14	18	7	10	10	27
Race or ethnicity							
White	29	14	24	7	10	16	29
Black	4	19	32	9	13	13	34
Hispanic	30	13	22	9	5	14	27[3]

1. Lacking desire for sex.
2. Arousal difficulties.
3. Inability to achieve climax or ejaculation.
4. Anxiety about sexual performance.
5. Climaxing or ejaculating too rapidly.
6. Physical pain during intercourse.
7. Not finding sex pleasurable.[4]

The advent of Viagra has focused attention on the physical causes of impotence, but the survey also associates it with stress, poverty, traumatic sexual events, and lack of education. For example, victims of rape or child molestation reported much higher rates of sexual dysfunction. Male victims of adult-child sexual contact were three times more likely to experience erectile dysfunction, and women who were "sexually forced" by a man were twice as likely to have arousal disorders.

Let's take a closer look:

Marital status—Whether someone is married has quite a bit to do with the incidence of sexual problems. Married women and men have a lower risk of experiencing sexual symptoms than unmarried people. The survey also found that unmarried women were one-and-a-half times more likely to suffer climax problems and sexual anxiety. Unmarried men reported much higher rates for most symptoms of sexual dysfunction.

Education—Women and men with lower levels of education reported that sex was less pleasurable and suffered higher levels of sexual anxiety. Women who were not high school graduates were approximately two times more likely to experience desire disorder, problems reaching orgasm, sexual pain, and sexual anxiety. Compared to men who are not high school graduates, college grads were only two-thirds as likely to report premature ejaculation and half as likely to report unsatisfactory sex and anxiety.

Race—Although the effects of race and ethnicity are fairly modest among both sexes, blacks appear more likely and Hispanics less likely to have sexual problems. Black women tend to have higher rates of low desire and pleasure, while white women are more likely to experience sexual pain. Hispanic women consistently reported fewer sexual problems. Differences among men were not as pronounced, although they generally were similar to what women reported.

Money—Declining household income was associated with a modest increase in risk for all areas of sexual dysfunction for women, but only erectile dysfunction for men.

Quality of Life—Sexual dysfunction generally is linked with poor quality of life, and it is more extensive and probably more severe for women than men.

Stress—Stress-related problems among men and women increase the risk of sexual difficulties in all phases of sexual response. The survey indicates that psychosocial difficulties affect sexuality, and that both physical and psychological factors are elements that affect sexual functioning.

Age—We have noted that the incidence of sexual problems for women tends to decrease with increasing age, except for those who have trouble lubricating. Increased age for men is associated with erection problems and lack of desire. The oldest group of men (fifty to fifty-nine) are more than three times as likely to experience erection and desire problems when compared with men eighteen to twenty-nine.

Trauma—Traumatic sexual acts have a great effect on sexuality, sometimes lasting far beyond the actual event. The impact is quite different for women than it is for men. Women respondents reporting same-sex activity are not at higher risk for sexual dysfunction while men are. Men reporting same-sex activity are more than twice as likely to experience low desire and premature ejaculation. Arousal disorder is very common among women who have experienced adult-child sexual contact. Men who have been victims of adult-child contact are three times as likely to experience erectile dysfunction and approximately two times as likely to experience premature ejaculation and diminished desire. The survey also shows that men who have sexually assaulted women are three-and-a-half times as likely to report erectile dysfunction.

The blues—The survey doesn't tell us whether bad sex causes the blues or the other way around. But correcting for other factors, women who had arousal problems were five times as likely to be unhappy with their lives as those with no sexual problems. Men with erectile problems were more than four times as likely to be unhappy.

Dr. Edward Laumann, lead author of the NHSLS and a sociology professor at the University of Chicago, not only was surprised by the extent of sexual dysfunction represented in his study, he also is convinced that the problem is even greater than his findings reveal. He believes that people are very reluctant to admit to impotence, including some of his test subjects. He and his colleagues agree, in their conclusion, that the results of the survey make it evident that sexual dysfunction is a significant public health concern.

DOING SOMETHING ABOUT IT

We now know impotence is a far more serious problem than previously suspected. And I'm pleased that we finally are facing the truth no matter how disturbing it is for us. But I remain concerned that the total number of cases is on the rise despite our expanding knowledge. Yes, the growing population of aging Americans is a factor, but the continued indiscriminate prescription of drugs for such conditions as hypertension and depression must be addressed. The declining quality of our diets and the increasing number of men and women who fail to exercise sufficiently also worry me.

In view of the tremendous number of sexual problems among us, it might seem foolish to be optimistic. But these are the best of times for doing something about it. Millions of previously silent men are going public, seeing doctors for the first time in years, and discovering other ailments that had gone undetected. Real hope exists for the majority of impotence sufferers, with effective treatment programs well within the budgets of most people. And although it might not seem like a breakthrough, the fact that you are reading about impotence is an important step toward finding solutions.

We know that sexual intimacy between loving people is a vital factor in achieving overall happiness. The loss of that closeness can cause tension at the very least, and at its worst can inflict irreparable damage. I want to emphasize that no one should suffer any form of sexual dysfunction without seeking help. The quickened pace of research, the rapid expansion of our knowledge, and a rush of scientific advances are providing us with solutions that shouldn't be ignored.

If you are experiencing problems that affect your sexuality, I recommend that you help yourself immediately by becoming better informed. Ignorance and myth have been our worst enemies in combating sexual dysfunction, but you can rectify that by studying some of the answers we have uncovered.

Help for Women

- Life without menopause? It's at least within the realm of possibility, thanks to research with mice. Scientists in Massachusetts have conducted tests that succeeded in silencing the gene that causes ovarian failure,[5] producing mice that are the equivalent of one hundred years old and possess active ovaries. Of course, not everybody wants to delay the onset of menopause.

- A supercervical hysterectomy, a fairly common procedure in Europe, removes the uterus but leaves the cervix intact. We've reached a point in this country where we should reevaluate routine removal of the cervix, which is known as a source of sexual pleasure, although it is a cancer risk.

- The clitoris, vagina, and uterus are now believed to be separate sources for orgasm. And women who are willing to practice, concentrate, and experiment are capable of improving their orgasmic reaction with the help of excellent books and videos or sessions with a sex therapist.

▓ Testosterone treatments can improve the intensity of female sexual gratification, and should be considered along with estrogen as a hormone replacement therapy for postmenopausal women. In a recent study a testosterone skin patch helped increase the sex drive of women with libido problems. More than half of the women tested with the patch reported an increase in desire.[6]

▓ We're still learning about the impact of hormones on female sexuality, but we know that estrogen therapy helps blood vessels relax and respond to exercise by increasing blood flow and keeping arteries reactive. There also is a growing belief that estrogen helps protect women against heart disease. All of which is good news for women and their sex lives.

Help for Men

▓ Viagra already has proved it is the answer for millions of men who suffer impotence. Sales have been phenomenal, and the majority of those who take it are satisfied. Tests on women also show positive results, and I believe it eventually will be used extensively by both sexes.

▓ Competitors for Viagra already are in various stages of research and should help bring down the price, which is about ten dollars a pill. I'm also sure Viagra and similar drugs will be sold over the counter some day.

▓ There are several other proven remedies for erectile dysfunction, which is good news for the thousands of men for whom Viagra is not a solution. Included is Muse, which is a suppository that can produce an erection when applied in the tip of the penis. Also effective are injection therapy, implants, vacuum pumps, testosterone treatment, and vascular surgery.

▓ Testicular cancer is fairly common among young men ages fifteen to thirty-five. In the early stages there usually are no symptoms other than a mass within the testicle, which makes routine self-inspection very important. The latest methods of treatment and early detection now yield a survival rate of more than 90 percent. However, many men don't examine themselves or are reluctant to reveal a problem.

■ According to the National Health and Social Life Survey, 29 percent of men experience premature ejaculation. Masters and Johnson contended that millions of men were troubled by it and that it was the most prevalent male sexual problem. There are a number of successful approaches to treating this disorder, including sex therapy.[7]

Help through Diet and Exercise

■ Many studies show that those who exercise regularly have greater ability to be aroused and to achieve orgasm. They also have higher levels of desire and greater sexual confidence. Exercise improves blood flow to all body parts, including reproductive organs.

■ Lack of exercise can lead to weight gain, which can result in diseases directly linked to impotence, including diabetes and hypertension. Exercise is known to contribute significantly to a feeling of well-being, an important element in our sex lives.

■ Soy products have ingredients that can reduce blood cholesterol levels as well as the risk of prostate cancer. Soy foods also are believed to be helpful in keeping hormones in balance. As the popularity of soy increases, food processors are coming up with more appetizing products, including flavored tofu and various vegetable blends.

■ The so-called "Mediterranean diet" emphasizes fruits, vegetables, grains, and fish, and has been proved effective in combating heart disease and other vascular problems. Also, research shows that cooking with olive oil and canola oil rather than other types of fats offers similar protection, which is a plus for sexual health.

■ Beware of those who tout high-protein, high-fat diets. Excess protein can be a factor in heart disease and other problems. We need protein in our diets, but you should select foods that provide the most nutritional benefits, such as substituting fish for meat and consuming various beans, peas, and lentils.

■ Ketchup, that old fast-food favorite, is better for you than you might realize. Tomato-based foods are loaded with lycopene, a powerful antioxidant, which according to the latest research plays a role in reducing the risk of cancer, including prostate cancer, a leading cause of impotence. According to the *Journal of the National Cancer Institute*, people who eat a lot of tomato products can reduce their risk of developing cancer by 40 percent.

- The evidence is mounting that carotenoids can reduce the possibility of heart disease, clogged arteries, and cancer. Carotenoids are found in many vegetables, including sweet potatoes, squash, and pumpkin. Cruciferous vegetables such as broccoli and Brussels sprouts are rich with beta-carotene, a carotenoid.

- High blood pressure can be reduced by consuming a combination of eight or nine servings of fruits and vegetables each day combined with three servings of low-fat dairy products.[8]

Before moving on, we need to talk about some aspects of impotence that are being pushed to the background by the Viagra frenzy. Yes, it seems miraculous that we now have a pill that can solve erectile dysfunction, arousal, and lubricating problems for many men and women. But we must understand that an erect penis and a stimulated clitoris do not guarantee happiness. That may seem elementary, but it has become popular in our culture to look for quick fixes, especially when it comes to sex.

Stable, pleasurable, and successful relationships are based more on trust, affection, and shared respect than on the ability to perform a sex act. While we are more aware than ever of physical causes of sexual dysfunction, we can't lose sight of the underlying seriousness of psychological problems. Viagra or other treatments might restore life to a formerly flaccid penis, but if the female partner is depressed, resentful, or angry, the pill loses its magic. Nobody should believe a rocky marriage is going to be saved by a pill.

I also want you to contemplate some truths before you begin exploring the detailed examination of impotence that follows.

You Need to Know

1   As you grow older, don't allow yourself to succumb to the belief that your sex life is coming to an end. Holding, touching, caressing, and kissing can go on forever, and as you move into the latter stages of life, intercourse remains within your capability even if it no longer is the necessity of your youth.

2   Basic changes in lifestyle at very little expense can help restore intimacy to a relationship. Actually, not drinking, not smoking, and eating fruits and vegetables instead of steaks and rich foods will save money as well as improve your sex life.

3   Impotence is not a sentence to life without sex. In most cases, it can be successfully treated. But the answers aren't always easy, and you must be open to the possibility that you and your partner might need professional help from your doctor and perhaps a sex therapist.

4   We have noted that if you or the person you love are suffering a sexual disorder, there is abundant help available. But most of us are capable of helping ourselves through aggressive self-education, effective communication, and a willingness to eliminate outdated notions about our sexuality.

Part II

WOMEN AND IMPOTENCE

Women and Impotence

T he news that there are 30 million impotent men in this country is stunning, but the revelation that 43 percent of American women are sexually dysfunctional, too, boggles the mind. Now take it a step further by adding to the equation the thousands of sexually capable women who have impotent husbands. That brings the actual dimensions of the problem into sharper focus.

Everybody, especially the male-dominated medical field, until now has failed to realize how widespread this problem is. Obviously, we need to sweep aside gender biases, ignorance, and Victorian prudishness and view this as a time of awakening and discovery. A good start would be to quit dancing around the term "female impotence."

In 1992, a paper published in the journal *Science* by Dr. Arthur L. Burnett and colleagues described a substance in the body called nitric oxide that is crucial to a penis becoming erect. Before that nobody fully understood the mechanism of erectile dysfunction. Now the same team has published another paper showing that nitric oxide also is produced in erectile tissue of a woman's reproductive system. The same kind of blood-flow problems that cause impotence in men can impair female sexual response as well. Blood must enter the vaginal area, especially the clitoris, for sexual responsiveness. Poor blood flow can cause poor orgasm, no orgasm, vaginal dryness, or other signs of limited stimulation. Everything that causes circulation problems in men also can apply to women. In fact, gender similarities are quite common when it comes to sex. The clitoris, for example, is much larger than previously thought and consists of a significant amount of erectile tissue, which, like the penis, becomes engorged with blood and swells during arousal.

Certain types of surgery also can cause impotence in women or diminished enjoyment. Now that we know more about the clitoris, the same nerve-saving techniques of prostate surgery should be applied to women. And the time probably has come to reevaluate the routine removal of the cervix with the rest of the uterus when hysterectomies are performed. In many women, the cervix is sensitive and adds to sexual pleasure, although it is susceptible to cancer. Supercervical hysterectomy, a practice more common in Europe, removes the uterus but leaves the cervix intact.

What we're finding out about female sexual anatomy gives us hope for combating dysfunction, but we are learning that the problem is more a matter of the mind for women than it is for men. Connie Engels—a certified sex therapist with the American Association of Sex Educators, Counselors, and Therapists—has contributed greatly to this section of the book and to my knowledge of impotence. Her expertise in the complicated area of female sexual response—and the psychological factors affecting it—has been particularly helpful. She has made it clear that doctors must do more than ask their female patients whether they can have intercourse and if it hurts when they do. She also has made it evident to me that joining forces with a qualified sex therapist would benefit most doctors.

Fortunately, we are rapidly expanding our knowledge of the complicated psychological factors that contribute to female sexual dysfunction. But, unfortunately, we also are finding it difficult to throw off the shackles of ancient theories and persistent myths that continue to inhibit women sexually.

Many children are being brought up in families that have unfortunate attitudes toward sex. Masturbation is regarded as a sin by many religions, and sexual activity of any kind during adolescence is the source of high anxiety among parents and teenagers alike. Feeling guilty about sex and denying their normal urges can negatively affect many women for their entire lives. So it is not surprising that when they move into a committed relationship, their sexuality is found to be significantly retarded.

Here's some good, basic advice for all of those who suffer from the mistakes of previous generations where sex is concerned. Ms. Engels recommends that you quit "working" at sex. Don't analyze your own performance while making love. Thoughts such as "Will I come?" "Am I lubricating?" or "Will it hurt?" can have disastrous results. Instead, concentrate on giving yourself permission to relax and enjoy being touched and stimulated. Also, don't be overly concerned about pleasing your partner. Please yourself, and learn more about your mind and body.

You Need to Know

1 Viagra for women could be the answer to blood-flow and lubrication problems. Some doctors are prescribing it already, although the drug may not have FDA approval for women for several years.

2 Physical and emotional abuse during childhood can affect sexuality in adulthood and lead to sexual dysfunction. Date rape is an example of an experience that also can have a negative effect later.

3 Many women are more interested in foreplay and afterplay than actual intercourse. Men usually want to get right to the main event, and afterplay is unknown to most of them.

4 Intercourse often does not result in orgasm for women, and multiple orgasms are even rarer. Clitoral touching, whether by masturbation or a partner, usually is more stimulating.

5 The loss of desire in postmenopausal women can be corrected with hormone replacement therapy, if a deficiency is the problem. Small doses of testosterone can have beneficial results.

Female Sexual Anatomy

- THE VULVA
- THE INNER STRUCTURE
- THE BREASTS

Women's bodies have been glorified, rhapsodized, and mythicized since the beginning of time, with great artists, writers, and composers endlessly applying their genius in adoration of the female form. And, of course, men's minds are bombarded with images of soft curves and alluring shapes, as if they need reminding.

Yet women too often fail to appreciate their physical attributes, remaining particularly ignorant of their marvelous reproductive structures. Sadly, too many little girls have been raised to shun certain portions of their bodies because they associate them with sin or impurity.

Let's put a stop to that *now* by carefully examining this miraculous machinery that brings life and pleasure to the world—when everything is working properly. Choose a tranquil and private moment in your busy day. Remove your clothing, sit on a high-backed chair, and hold a small mirror at an angle that gives a clear view of the external components of your sex organs. Gently use your fingers to gain an appreciation for texture and design, then take your time and enjoy the experience as I describe what you are seeing.

THE VULVA

The vulva encompasses the external genitals, including the mons veneris, labia majora, labia minora, clitoris, and urinary and vaginal openings. The vulva differs in appearance among individual people, and it has been described as looking like certain flowers and other natural forms.[9]

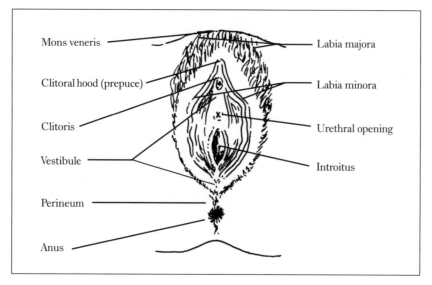

Vulva

Mons Veneris—The mons is the area that covers the pubic bone. It consists of pads of fatty tissue between the bone and the skin. There are many nerve endings present in the mons, making it an area that produces sexual pleasure.

Labia Majora—They are commonly referred to as the "outer lips," and extend down from the mons on each side of the vulva. Beginning next to the thigh, they extend inward and surround the labia minora and the vaginal and urethral openings. The skin of the labia majora is usually darker than the skin of the thighs, and the underlying fatty tissue and nerve endings are much like those of the mons.

Labia Minora—These "inner lips" are located inside the outer lips and often protrude between them. They are hairless folds of skin that join at the clitoral hood and extend down past the urinary and vaginal openings. They contain oil and sweat glands, many blood vessels, as well as nerve endings. They also vary in size, shape, and color among individuals.

The Clitoris—We now know that the clitoris extends deep into the body and that its size is at least twice as large as most anatomy texts indicate. Studies by Dr. Helen O'Connell, who is a urologist at the Royal Melbourne Hospital in Melbourne, Australia, reveal that the clitoris actually extends more than three inches into the body in a pyramid of tissue whose sole function is to give sexual pleasure.[10] O'Connell's studies include an examination of the nerves and blood vessels that serve the clitoris, allowing it to swell and engorge during sexual arousal in much the same way the penis does in men. Those vital connections are in danger of being severed when women undergo some types of pelvic surgery, thus diminishing their sexual arousal or ability to have orgasms. O'Connell also found that the clitoris is much closer to the urethra than previously thought. The clitoris surrounds it on three sides, making it vulnerable during surgery. She also found that the erectile tissue of the clitoris encompasses a much larger area of the anterior vaginal wall than previously thought.[11] She believes this clearly indicates that erectile dysfunction is a problem for women as well as men. I believe the clitoris probably hasn't been accurately measured in the past because the bulk of it is hidden beneath the pubic bone and under fat. The basic structure of the clitoris includes the external shaft and glands as well as the internal crura (roots), which project inward from each side of the clitoral shaft. The shaft and glans are located where the inner lips converge, just below the mons area. They are covered by the clitoral hood. The shaft contains two small spongy structures called the cavernous bodies, which engorge with blood during sexual arousal. These become the crura as they connect to the pubic bones in the pelvic cavity. The glans often is not visible under the clitoral hood, but it can be seen by gently parting the labia minora and retracting the hood. The appearance of the glans is smooth, rounded, and slightly translucent. The external part of the clitoris has approximately the same number of nerve endings as the head of the penis and is highly sensitive. The size, shape, and position of the clitoris vary among women.

The Vestibule—It is the area of the vulva located inside the labia minora and contains an extensive system of blood vessels and nerve endings. Its tissue is very sensitive to the touch. The urinary and vaginal openings are located within the vestibule.

The Urethral Opening—Urine passes out of a woman's body through the urethral opening. The urethra is the tube connecting the bladder to the urinary opening. It is located between the clitoris and the vaginal opening.

The Introitus and Hymen—The introitus is the opening of the vagina, which is situated between the urinary opening and the anus. Covering part of the introitus is a fold of tissue called the hymen, which is present at birth and usually remains intact until coitus occurs. The hymen possibly serves to protect vaginal tissue, but it has no other known function. However, many people have placed great significance on its presence or its absence, believing that a woman's virginity can be proved by the pain and bleeding that may occur with the initial coitus. Actually, this is not always true, and in some cases the hymen may remain intact after intercourse.

The Perineum—This is the area of smooth skin situated between the vaginal opening and the anus. The perineal tissue contains nerve endings and is sensitive to the touch. Physicians sometimes make an incision called an episiotomy in the perineum to prevent the tearing of tissues as a newborn passes through the birth canal.

THE INNER STRUCTURE

Included in the internal female sexual anatomy are the vagina, cervix, uterus, fallopian tubes, and ovaries.

The Vagina—It is a canal that opens between the labia minora and extends into the body, extending up toward the small of the back to the cervix and uterus. In a nonaroused state, the vagina is approximately three to five inches long. The walls form a flat tube that can expand and serve as a birth passage. The vagina also changes in size and shape during sexual activity. There are three layers of tissue in the vagina—mucous, muscle, and fibrous—which contain many blood vessels. The mucosa is the layer of mucous lining that a woman feels when she inserts a finger inside her vagina. The folded walls (rugae) produce secretions that help maintain the chemical balance of the vagina. During sexual arousal, a lubricating substance exudes through the mucosa. Most of the second layer, composed of muscle tissue, is concentrated near the vaginal opening. Surrounding the muscular layer is the deepest vaginal layer, which is composed of fibrous tissue. This layer has a role in vaginal contraction and expansion, and acts as connective tissue to other structures in the pelvic cavity.

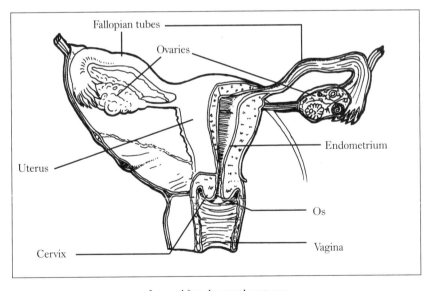

Internal female sexual anatomy

The Cervix—It is located at the upper portion of the vagina and is the lower part of the uterus. It contains mucus-secreting glands. Sperm pass through the vagina into the uterus through the os, the opening in the center of the cervix. A woman can feel her cervix by inserting a finger into the vagina and reaching to the end of the canal. It feels somewhat firm and round in contrast to the soft vaginal walls.

The Uterus—It is a hollow organ, and is approximately three inches long and two inches wide in a woman who never has given birth. The uterus is suspended in the pelvic cavity by ligaments. The walls of the uterus include three layers. The external layer is a thin membrane called the perimetrium. The middle layer, myometrium, is made of muscle fibers that enable the uterus to stretch during pregnancy and contract during labor and orgasm. At the top of the uterus, an area called the fundus, the uterine walls are especially thick. The inner lining of the uterus is called the endometrium, which has many blood vessels and sustains the "zygote" (united sperm and egg), which travels down to the uterus from the fallopian tubes after fertilization. The endometrium also is a source of hormone production.

The Fallopian Tubes—Each of the fallopian tubes extends from the uterus toward the ovary, at the left or the right side of the pelvic cavity. The outside end of each tube is shaped like a funnel, with projections called "fimbrae." When the egg leaves the ovary, it is drawn into the tube by the fimbrae. Once the egg is inside the tube, the movements of tiny, hairlike "cilia" and the contractions of the tube walls move it along at a rate of approximately one inch about every twenty-four hours. The egg is viable for fertilization for up to forty-eight hours. Fertilization occurs while the egg is in the outer one-third of the tube. After fertilization, the zygote begins developing as it travels down the tube to the uterus.

The Ovaries—The two ovaries are about the size and shape of almonds and are located at the ends of the fallopian tubes, one on each side of the uterus. They are connected to the pelvic wall and the uterus by ligaments. The ovaries are endocrine glands that produce two classes of sex hormones. The estrogens influence development of female physical sex characteristics and help regulate the menstrual cycle. The progestational compounds also help regulate the menstrual cycle and promote maturity of the uterine lining in preparation for pregnancy. Around the onset of puberty, the female sex hormones play an important role in initiating maturation of the uterus, ovaries, and vagina, and in the development of the secondary sex characteristics such as pubic hair and breasts. The ovaries contain up to four hundred thousand immature ova, which are present at birth. During the years between puberty and menopause, one or the other ovary typically releases an egg during each cycle. Ovulation occurs as the result of the complex chain of events known as the menstrual cycle.

THE BREASTS

We include a woman's breasts in this discussion because they are a secondary sex characteristic, as are body hair and a deep voice in men. More importantly, I want to change some notions women have about their breasts as well as promote self-examination by all women to protect themselves against cancer.

Fed by buxom images in the media, many people in our society have had a preoccupation with size, somehow linking large breasts with sex appeal. Personally, I sometimes have concern about implants being placed in such a vulnerable part of the body merely for enhancement, but at one time 150,000 women a year were doing it.

We have conditioned too many women to believe that their breasts are too small, too big, or even poorly shaped. I've heard it all. Some patients have been haunted since puberty because they thought their breasts were too small. Others are just as self-conscious because they see them as too big. It's a shame that anyone believes breast *size* is the prime turn-on for men, most of whom will tell you that female allure is far more complicated than that.

The breasts are composed internally of fatty tissue and mammary glands, and size is determined mostly by the quantity of fatty tissue present. One breast is commonly a different size than the other. Breasts also show some size variations during the menstrual cycle or when pregnancy or nursing is involved. The darker area of the breast is called the areola, and in the center of that is the nipple, which becomes erect during arousal or when stimulated by touching.

I also believe that any discussion of the breasts must go beyond sexual aspects. Self-examination of your breasts is extremely important, and the best time to do it is after menstruation because of cyclic changes in the breast tissue. Become familiar with your breasts and report any changes to your doctor. Ninety percent of breast lumps, most of which are not malignant, are found by women themselves.

A possible breakthrough in the treatment of breast cancer was reported in June 1999. A study reported in the *Journal of the American Medical Association* found that a drug approved to fight the bone disease osteoporosis significantly decreased the risk of breast cancer among postmenopausal women. The drug, raloxifene (Evista), reduced the risk of breast cancer by 76 percent among women who took it compared with those who took a dummy pill. The study was conducted over a period of three years by a team led by Dr. Steven R. Cummings of the University of California at San Francisco.

The American Society of Clinical Oncology cautioned that it is premature to recommend raloxifene to lower the risk of breast cancer except in clinical trials. It pointed out that it remains to be seen whether the benefit is long lasting. Dr. Cummings, on the other hand, said, "The results were quite dramatic, and we do not often see this amount of preventive medicine."

Last year the Food and Drug Administration approved the drug tamoxifen as a cancer preventive for postmenopausal women at high risk of developing the disease. I find the advances with tamoxifen and the raloxifene findings very encouraging. But I will be quite interested in seeing the results of a trial under way that compares the effectiveness of the two drugs among twenty-two thousand women in four hundred medical centers in the United States and Canada.[12]

Although we are witnessing a remarkable surge in research and development of drugs, all women should remember that there is no substitute for self-examination, having a mammogram every year or two (every year for women over fifty), and an annual examination by a physician. Taking these steps significantly reduces the chances of a woman dying of breast cancer.

You Need to Know

Breast cancer is the leading cause of cancer death in women between the ages of forty and fifty-five. Approximately 180,000 new cases occur each year in the United States. The five-year survival rate from localized breast cancer has increased to 97 percent.

Endometrial cancer of the uterus is the most common type of cancer that develops in the pelvic area in women. About thirty-five thousand new cases are diagnosed in the United States each year.

The American Cancer Society estimated that there were 25,400 new cases of ovarian cancer in 1998, with 14,500 deaths. It most frequently affects older women with a peak incidence in the mid-fifties.

There are sixteen thousand cases of invasive cervical cancer each year in the United States. If every woman would get an annual Pap test, the incidence of invasive cervical cancer would drop dramatically and would, in fact, be nearly eliminated.[13]

Female Sexuality

- ORGASM DEFINED
- LEARNING BY TOUCH
- HORMONES AND SEX
- MENOPAUSE

There are many assumptions about women in Western culture that just won't go away, although some negative stereotypes are slowly fading. One mistaken belief handed down through the generations is that women are less interested in sex than men, and a lot of people still think that sex for a woman is a matter of pleasing a man rather than her own enjoyment. Others remain convinced that it is wrong for a woman to be aroused or to respond sexually.

The expectation lingering in our society that women play a passive role leaves most of them angry and frustrated, especially when they ponder the myth that men are more knowledgeable about sex. Even in this high-tech age of enlightenment, we have much to learn about sexuality, especially when it comes to women.

A man's ability to have an erection has been a hot research topic for several years, but our understanding of female response lags far behind. Blame our prudish culture, blame the women who are too embarrassed to talk about it, blame the medical profession, but the reality is that most of us are repressed and uninformed about our own sexuality. This point is validated by the patients who tell me they've never had an orgasm and aren't sure they would recognize one if they did.

We are just beginning to evaluate female arousal, but there are some things we know. How a woman feels sexually can depend not only on her upbringing, age, stress level, and happiness with a partner, but also on daily hormone fluctuations. Women also experience a greater variety of response patterns than men. For example, after orgasm, men pretty much shut down for awhile. Women, on the other hand, are capable of multiple orgasms, although few actually experience them.

When discussing sex, we always must recognize the tremendous individual variances in both genders, but especially in women. We also must understand that the tie between mind and body is so powerful that medical problems can become emotional ones, particularly with women. For example, heavy use of antihistamines and other medications can lead to vaginal dryness, causing painful intercourse, thus killing desire.

ORGASM DEFINED

A scientist would say orgasm is the peaking of pleasure with release of sexual tension and rhythmic contractions of the perineal muscles, anal sphincter, and pelvic reproductive organs. Moviemakers and fiction writers prefer far more dramatic but less accurate descriptions ...

> "Phenomenal! Ecstasy! Fireworks."
> "It's like eating a hot fudge sundae."
> "It's like going to heaven."
> "I'm overwhelmed by more pleasure than I've ever felt."
> "I float in another realm of consciousness."

Need we say more? Yes!

Connie Engels, our sex therapist, explains that through the years women often have felt inadequate because their own experience with orgasm hasn't matched the exaggerated descriptions they have read in works of fiction—written mostly by men. Some women may experience very intense orgasms, but that is not the norm for the average female.

With more research and better communication, we now recognize their wide variety of experiences with orgasm, few of which amount to "lights exploding" or "heavenly sensations." Here are some more appropriate descriptions:

"A pleasurable feeling."
"A feeling of delicious warmth."
"A strong sense of release of tension."
"A mild sense of well-being."
"A feeling of relaxation."

Usually when women start having orgasms they may well be very subtle, but with more practice and concentration, they can become more intense. Ms. Engels recommends that you experiment with your body and arrive at your own definition of an orgasm. Take your time. Don't allow yourself to be discouraged, and realize that this is not a simple process with quick solutions. And if you feel in need of help, ask for it. There are a number of books and videotapes on the market that will take you through various steps leading to an understanding of what happens during orgasm. (see page 67.)

Set aside thirty to forty-five minutes in a pleasant setting. Do some relaxation exercises, treat yourself to a bubble bath, light candles, put on some soft music. Use some oil or lotion and explore your body. Follow our earlier suggestion that you use a mirror to look at your genitalia and identify the various parts, including the clitoris. Then proceed to touching and pleasuring your body, exploring the areas that arouse you the most.

You will learn some techniques in achieving arousal, but mostly you will discover how to touch and how to be touched. Women react in different ways to these exercises. Some may be afraid, others are curious, and still others are repulsed or feel guilty and anxious. But a lot of you will become excited.

Go slowly, focusing on self-discovery. Do some more relaxation breathing, give yourself permission to enjoy. Use sexual fantasies, visualize an erotic scene in a movie, or remember a special passage from a book. Slow down, then try some role-playing and pretend you are having an orgasm, move around, make some noise, cry out. You're learning!

Next time practice some orgasm triggers:

- When aroused, tense your legs, feet, and stomach.

- Body tension can increase sexual tension and trigger an orgasm.

- When you feel aroused, try teasing yourself.

- Watch yourself in a mirror.

- Wear sexy underwear.

- Try really letting go. Move your hips and body.

You must learn that *you* are responsible for your own sexuality, and after you have learned more about yourself, you must teach your partner. Success will depend greatly on how willing you are to open yourself up, how flexible you are about lovemaking styles and techniques. Be sensual. Be passionate.

Many women are capable of self-education, but I recommend working through the process with the assistance of a certified sex therapist. It helps to have someone to share your feelings and reactions and to assist you if you get stuck. It also helps to be realistic about orgasms and their importance to your lovemaking. Professional sex therapists do not consider having an orgasm to be critical to the enjoyment of sex, although many women are concerned that they cannot have multiple orgasms, or that they cannot have simultaneous coital orgasms. Women usually do not experience orgasms during intercourse because the stimulation of penile thrusting is not direct enough to cause it. The absence of orgasm with intercourse *is not* a sexual dysfunction. Multiple orgasms *do not* occur frequently. There are some women who never experience orgasm or do so only after prolonged stimulation.

My knowledge of the physiology of female sexual response has expanded significantly in recent years. For example, we believe there are three separate sources for orgasms—the clitoris, the vagina, and the uterus. We also know that Dr. Freud's theory that vaginal orgasm was more mature and preferable than clitoral orgasm is all wet, although it has had a lingering effect. His theories led women to believe that clitoral stimulation was a "masculine" act, and psychotherapy was recommended to help attain vaginal orgasms, supposedly a more feminine expression.

You can imagine what this did to women who enjoyed stimulation of the clitoris. Freud's teachings sometimes led to some practitioners recommending that the clitoris be surgically removed in girls who masturbated to help them eventually attain "vaginal" orgasms.

You Need to Know

1 The Grafenberg Spot, an area along the anterior wall of the vagina, also is believed to be a source of orgasm with vigorous stimulation.

2 Current evidence suggests some stimulation of the clitoris is essential to having an orgasm.

3 Masters and Johnson described four phases in sexual response patterns: excitement, plateau, orgasm, and resolution.

4 Orgasm lasts a little longer in women than men and is marked by involuntary muscle spasms throughout the body. Blood pressure, heart rate, and respiration increase.

5 Touch, of all the senses, has the most to do with sexual arousal. And the areas that produce the most pleasure when touched are called the erogenous zones.

Learning by Touch

> Touch is an end in itself. It is a primary form of communication, a silent voice that avoids the pitfall of words while expressing the feelings of the moment. It bridges the physical separateness from which no human being is spared, literally establishing a sense of solidarity between two individuals. Touching is sensual pleasure, exploring the textures of skin, the suppleness of muscle, the contours of the body, with no further goal than enjoyment of tactile perceptions.
>
> —Masters and Johnson[14]

We come into this world with a dramatic rush punctuated by startling sensations, pacified finally by one stimulation—touch. It is such an important sense that a baby deprived of it could become ill or grow up to be maladjusted. The entire surface of our bodies is a sensory organ, and touching it almost anywhere can give security to a child and enhance intimacy in adults. A relationship deprived of the warmth of a caress and the thrill of exploring fingertips is in great danger of failure.

Beth[15] wanted nothing more than to be held and kissed. She understood the effect of radical prostate surgery on her husband, but Ray was devastated by what he thought was the end of his once-active sex life. He refused to touch his wife if he couldn't produce an erection, and both of them were depressed.

After two years of Beth begging Ray to at least hold her, then threatening to have an affair, their marriage was on the brink of divorce. As a last resort, he reluctantly agreed to see a urologist about the possibilities of a penile implant. This doctor did the right thing, insisting that *together* they see a sex therapist before proceeding with surgery.

Initially, the therapy centered on the pros and cons of the surgery and the reactions of *both* of them. The next step was to begin breaking down the barriers that were keeping them from being close. Sensate focus touching exercises were assigned as homework over a period of about two months. Videotapes and books were included to increase their understanding of sexuality in general.

Beth and Ray had been rather restricted in their previous lovemaking, but through the process of therapy they decided to be more creative and expand their repertoire. They soon discovered how much pleasure they could give each other without intercourse being a factor. Eventually reconnected emotionally and with fully developed lovemaking skills, they decided an implant wasn't necessary.

Sensate Focus Exercises

Researchers Masters and Johnson introduced sensate focus exercises as a way to achieve sexual enrichment for couples with intimacy problems. Connie Engels recommends them for those who want to solve nonphysical erectile difficulties and to boost orgasmic response. She also sees these exercises as a way to relearn the basics of being affectionate and of receiving pleasure from their partners.

Most of us have learned what we know about affectionate touch within our families, and the result is that some of us are more touch oriented than are others. When these divergent views come together in a marriage, there often is conflict, but people can restore closeness to a relationship by learning how to touch and be touched.

Sensate focus exercises are designed to help a couple develop a heightened awareness of sensations rather than performance by emphasizing the enjoyment of touching rather than the anxiety of striving toward erection or orgasm. Partners are encouraged to approach changes in their physical and emotional involvement in a gradual way and in a shared, nonthreatening environment.

There is excellent reading material available that explains in detail the proper procedures of sensate focus, but assistance from a sex therapist is the recommended way to get the most out of these exercises. Educate yourself by reading what Masters and Johnson have to say, but rely on an expert to guide you through the process.

HORMONES AND SEX

Dad's call was such a surprise because my mother always had been a calm, stabilizing influence in our family. Now I was hearing that she was in a psychiatric hospital suffering a nervous breakdown. She was depressed, cried constantly, couldn't sleep, felt nervous all the time, and they were ready to try electric shock therapy.

It was 1956, and my mother had turned fifty-two. I was in medical school, already developing an interest in gynecology. My curiosity inspired a lot of outside reading on the subject, and I'm sure I made a pest of myself asking the faculty a lot of questions. But what I already knew made me suspicious as I drove home, worried about my mother, but already thinking that I had an answer.

After being ushered into the locked ward, I asked her a few questions and did a lot of listening. Her overworked family practitioner had done what a lot of doctors did with women at the time, attributing her behavior to "mental problems." I knew better. She was menopausal and was *not* having a nervous collapse.

What passed for estrogen replacement in those days had her back to normal in a few weeks, and I knew what I was going to do with the rest of my life. The answers don't always come so easily when hormones are involved, and we're just beginning to make some connections between them and sexuality. But it's very important for women of all ages to understand hormones and their effect on them.

Basically, the gonads in our bodies produce hormones and secrete them directly into the bloodstream. Ovaries produce estrogens, which influence female physical characteristics and help regulate the menstrual cycle. The primary hormone products of the testes are androgens, the most important being testosterone, which influences male physical sex characteristics *as well as sexual motivation*. Hormones also are secreted by the adrenal glands, including estrogen and androgens *in both sexes*. Women should be aware that the ovaries also produce androgens, including testosterone, although far less than in men.

We know that estrogen is involved in vaginal lubrication and enhances elasticity of the vaginal lining, but it's unclear whether it has anything to do with sexual motivation. A recent study of postmenopausal women and women who had their ovaries surgically removed and underwent estrogen replacement therapy showed increased pleasure and capacity for orgasm. At the same time, other studies have found no impact at all on desire and activity with estrogen replacement. We have a lot to learn.

Androgens, testosterone specifically, are another story. We don't fully understand all that is involved in sexual desire, but there are indications that testosterone modulates neurotransmitters in the central nervous system, which then play a role in boosting libido. Studies going as far back as the sixties show that testosterone treatments can increase the susceptibility to sexual stimulation, increase genitalia sensitivity, and improve the intensity of female sexual gratification. This has been a neglected area of medicine that I believe deserves increased attention. All women who have undergone surgical menopause should be asked about their sexual activity, and testosterone in addition to estrogen should be considered if they cite decreased libido. The dual treatment also should be considered for naturally menopausal women who complain of decreased libido.

Psychological factors must be part of the evaluation, too. We do know that estrogen in hormone replacement therapy can enhance a woman's feelings of well-being by reducing the effects of depression and hot flashes. It also can alleviate problems such as insomnia and anxiety caused by estrogen deficiency.

Much less is known about the relationship between hormones and female sexuality than it is for men. And we should be aware that all human sexual behavior is highly individualized, which complicates our understanding of exactly how hormones impact erotic arousal and expression. We also must remember that problems such as stress, exhaustion, depression, and body image have an effect on libido.

Before we move on to another subject, I must say that I have never understood why so many people have avoided hormone therapy because they fear a connection with breast cancer. A study published on June 10, 1999, in the *Journal of the American Medical Association* should put to rest those concerns.

The research, involving thirty-seven thousand women over an eleven-year period, found that taking hormones after menopause *does not* increase the risk of breast cancer. The only exceptions would be some uncommon forms of the disease that are slow growing and highly treatable.

"When a woman weighs the risk of breast cancer versus the benefit of possibly reducing cardiovascular disease and reducing risk of osteoporosis, this just provides further evidence for the benefit," said Dr. Susan M. Gapstur, a cancer epidemiologist at Northwestern University Medical School, who led the study and is quoted in the *JAMA* article.

You Need to Know

1 Estrogen is a hormone made by a woman's body, mainly in the ovaries. It allows her to have children and helps keep her bones strong. Many scientists think that estrogen also helps protect women against heart disease.

2 Several population studies have shown that the loss of natural estrogen as women age may contribute to a higher risk of coronary heart disease in women after menopause. That's when the body's production of estrogen starts to decline.

3 If you have had a natural or surgical menopause, you may be considering estrogen or hormone therapy. ERT is either a natural or a synthetic form of estrogen that can be taken in a pill, by injection, a patch, a pellet, or topical cream. HRT is estrogen therapy combined with a progestin for women with an intact uterus. Women who have had their uterus removed (a hysterectomy) may not need progestin and can take ERT alone.

4 Other research has shown that estrogen therapy helps blood vessels relax and respond to exercise and physical stress by keeping arteries reactive and by increasing blood flow. ERT and HRT help relieve symptoms of menopause, protect against the bone disease osteoporosis, and help prevent fractures. Early clinical data have shown that the loss of estrogen in women is linked to risk of Alzheimer's disease. The disease may be less likely to strike women who take estrogen after menopause.

5 ERT (estrogen alone) raises the risk of endometrial or uterine cancer in women with an intact uterus. However, HRT (combining estrogen and progestin) reduces the increased risk of endometrial cancer. There is a slightly higher risk of thrombophlebitis and a higher risk of gallbladder disease in women taking ERT or HRT.[16]

MENOPAUSE

> The classical medical terminology for menopause is *ovarian failure*. Another way of seeing it would be as *ovarian fulfillment*. One has put in thirty or forty years of ripening eggs and enduring the hormonal mischief of monthly cycles on the chance that a child is wanted. Enough, say most women in middle age. We're ready to move on now, to find our place in the world, free of the responsibilities of our procreative years. It's time to take risks and pursue passions and allow ourselves adventures perhaps set aside way back at thirteen, when we accepted the cultural script for our gender that ordinarily denied those dreams. It's time to play! And kick up some dust![17]
>
> —Gail Sheehy

Thanks to misinformation and ignorance, many women approach this time in their lives with trepidation, but the truth is many of them breeze right through it, experiencing little more than the usually welcome end to menstruation. Finally free of anxiety about pregnancy and contraception, they discover intimacy without apprehension.

Now, as the century turns, powerful forces are inspiring the nation's health-care system to pay more attention to menopause and to expand its understanding of how the aging process impacts female sexuality. The impetus is coming from 40 million postmenopausal women, who today have a life expectancy of eighty, as well as the influential Baby Boomer generation, which is beginning to swell the ranks of the middle-aged.

The effects of menopause differ greatly among individuals, most of whom experience only minor changes sexually. Some women suffer a decline in interest, excitement, and orgasms, but hormone replacement therapy, sex therapy, and improved research can resolve many sexual problems experienced by older women.

This change in a woman's body may begin around the age of forty when the ovaries begin to produce less estrogen. About ten years later menstruation ceases, and menopause takes place naturally, the exception being when the ovaries are surgically removed for health reasons.

Generally, the sexual response cycle of most women continues to occur but with somewhat decreased intensity because of the hormonal changes. A number of studies of women in their fifties find that most of them don't experience problems with arousal, desire, or satisfaction, although those with very low estrogen levels do tend to be less active sexually.

But let's face it, there are changes that *do* take place in the sexuality of older women.

It will take longer before vaginal lubrication takes place, and the amount probably will be reduced.

- The decrease in estrogen changes urethral tissues, which lose tone and become affected by dryness. That can lead to infections or the patient can develop urinary incontinence. Vaginal mucosa becomes thinner, and the length and width of the vagina decreases.

- In older women, orgasmic contractions continue to occur although typically fewer in number. In some postmenopausal women, uterine contractions can be painful.

- In one respected study, 69 percent of women ages sixty to ninety-one listed orgasm first when asked what they considered to be a satisfying sexual encounter. Only 12 percent answered "intercourse."[18]

- Vaginal changes because of aging are less pronounced in women who are active sexually.

- There are excellent topical vaginal estrogens and moisturizers that alleviate problems with vaginal dryness. Exercise and good nutrition also are recommended for menopausal symptoms.

The desire for love, affection, and intimacy does not end at any age. But there are inhibiting factors such as depression caused either by illness or a lack of sexual activity because of a partner's inability. Feeling locked into an unhappy relationship certainly can affect libido, too. And some people are still coming to terms with the fact that sexual behavior continues into old age. Stereotypes characterizing men as aggressive and women as passive sexually are unchanging and no doubt limit sexual behavior of older women. And, finally, there are a number of physicians who are reluctant to inquire about libido in postmenopausal women, which is unfortunate because we now have so many solutions.

You Need to Know

Older couples may find themselves capable of enjoying sex more than ever. Concerns about children, work, and achieving success diminish, paving the way for more relaxed lovemaking.

Longer periods of intimacy, including kisses, embraces, and caresses, can typify relationships in later years. Frequency of intercourse sometimes *increases* as a couple grows older.

Many older couples find that they enjoy sex more even if they have sex less frequently. They are more willing to experiment with various forms of stimulation, including options beyond intercourse.

Sexual drive varies greatly among individuals, but sexuality is an important factor in the lives of most older people.

Female Sexual Dysfunction

- DESIRE DISORDER
- AROUSAL DISORDER
- ORGASMIC DISORDER
- OTHER PROBLEMS

Phil brought his wife to a sex therapist because he had lost all patience with her refusal to have sex with him. She had, at his insistence, seen a gynecologist who treated her with testosterone, but her interest in her husband did not improve. Phil thought therapy would be the answer, and it was, to his chagrin.

While taking a family history, it was discovered that Phil had a drinking problem, and, according to his wife, had been insensitive toward her for years. Therapy also revealed that she was very angry and had no desire for sex with him—or anyone else.

He denied the drinking problem and continued to blame his wife for their deteriorating relationship. Finally, his inability to assume responsibility for his abuse of alcohol or anything else troubling the couple prevented therapy from progressing, and he went elsewhere to "fix" his wife's low-desire problem. You can't be optimistic about the future of that marriage.

Clearly, the lesson here is that individual issues must be addressed before a couple can move on toward improved lovemaking. Understanding the lack of desire on the part of Phil's wife is relatively easy, but there are innumerable individual variables and many complicated factors that are known to contribute to female sexual dysfunction.

DESIRE DISORDER

Defining sexual desire is a challenge unless you accept the old definition that it is instinctive, something you are born with. The latest research serves mostly to point out how complicated this aspect of sexuality is, especially as it pertains to women. After all, how do you measure "low" levels of desire, or what is "normal" desire? But it's safe to describe it as an energizing force that motivates a person to seek genital sexual sensations.

Discrepancy in desire levels between men and women is the most reported sexual difficulty involving couples. And, typically, women are the victims of this disorder, often responding by feeling inadequate or worrying too much about their lack of desire. When you combine these factors with a partner whose level of desire is high, serious conflict usually occurs.

Some women who have a desire disorder are capable of becoming aroused and can experience orgasm if sufficiently stimulated. Others may be tense and anxious rather than aroused by sexual contact. A woman with this disorder at times sees sex with her partner as an obligatory function, part of the marital contract. There also are women who develop an extreme aversion to sex, which can be the result of trauma or abuse.

Lifelong cases of the disorder are rare, and usually people develop it at a specific point in their lives. It normally isn't seen as a serious problem unless it causes distress in a relationship. There are multiple possible causes and influences concerning desire, and usually there is no single reason for low levels. Some factors include:

1. Sexual phobias
2. Fear of loss of control
3. Fear of pregnancy
4. Sexual deviation issues
5. Performance anxiety
6. Inadequate grieving after the death of a loved one
7. Hormone deficiencies
8. Medication side effects or serious illness
9. Homosexual or bisexual conflicts
10. Aging-related changes and concerns
11. Religious orthodoxy teachings
12. Obsessive-compulsive personality problems
13. Depression
14. Sexual trauma, rape
15. Conflict in the marital relationship

Therapists believe this is the most complicated sexual disorder to treat. The initial goal probably would be to help modify a person's tendency to inhibit erotic impulses and to understand the underlying motivation for suppressing sexuality.

AROUSAL DISORDER

Women who have arousal problems commonly experience a lack of vaginal lubrication, which normally is the initial response to sexual stimulation. Typically, a woman with this disorder doesn't feel erotic sensations, and in fact she may find sex only slightly enjoyable or even repulsive. For some women, lack of lubrication can be an occasional problem, but there are others who never have experienced it when having sex.

Among the common causes of arousal dysfunction are apathy, anger, fear, and guilt. Guilt usually involves an internal conflict between a desire to enjoy sexual interaction and an unconscious fear of doing so. Anger often involves a woman's partner. Biological factors also can be the source, including low estrogen levels. But keep in mind the fact that most of us don't respond sexually all the time. The demands of a hectic lifestyle can diminish anyone's arousal capability. And lack of lubrication in certain situations doesn't necessarily mean there is a problem. Difficulties also could be the failure to communicate to a partner the specific techniques that produce excitement. But if there is a chronic absence of arousal or erotic sensations, getting some professional help is recommended.

ORGASMIC DISORDER

Anorgasmia is the term used by sex educators and therapists to describe absence of orgasm in women. Those who have this problem can be very sexually aroused but never reach orgasm. Some women experience orgasm rarely or only in some situations and not others. An example of the latter would be someone who reaches orgasm through masturbation but not in response to her partner's stimulation.

Although many women are satisfied with their sexual experience without orgasm, others are distressed and disappointed, which can lead to serious difficulties. Only in rare cases does anorgasmia have a physiological cause such as medications or certain physical conditions that affect the vascular system or nerve supply.

Not having orgasm during intercourse without simultaneous stimulation of the clitoris is the *normal* pattern of millions of women. According to the American Psychiatric Association, "Women exhibit wide variability in the type of intensity of stimulation that triggers orgasm. The diagnosis of female orgasmic disorder should be based on the clinician's judgment that the woman's orgasmic capacity is less than would be reasonable for her age, sexual experience, and the adequacy of sexual stimulation that she receives."

A common cause of the disorder is our undue emphasis on intercourse and orgasm as the goal for sex, which leads to pressure and often precludes orgasm. And there also are women who haven't tried to find out what arouses them, or for a variety of reasons they avoid becoming aroused enough to climax. Hostility toward a woman's partner and "withholding" her orgasm to punish him would be an example.

I must note here that ineffective sexual technique also can contribute to anorgasmia. Making love requires a learned talent for pleasurable stimulation, and some people fail to realize that they should make a conscious effort to improve on their methods of producing pleasure. Unfortunately, anxiety, family problems, or acquired inhibitions can cause women to shun effective stimulation.

Betty, who was shy and had done little dating, was married as a college sophomore. She and Mark had become sexually involved before the wedding, and throughout their lovemaking he had tried to bring her to orgasm, but to no avail.

She at first told him not to worry about her, but in time she became increasingly frustrated and usually ended up crying after they had sex. He, in response, began to feel guilty that he couldn't make it happen. But their marriage somehow survived a long period of unsatisfactory sexual intimacy, although they gradually withdrew emotionally from each other. Eventually, Betty became deeply depressed and sought professional help. This soon led them to therapy together, where they finally began to address the problems that had developed between them.

They worked hard on setting aside time for each other, went on dates, talked more, practiced just kissing and holding each other. Then Betty worked with a sex therapist on accepting her own sexuality, reaching a point where she could have an orgasm through self-masturbation with a vibrator. Mark joined her in this activity, and with the guidance of the therapist, she took responsibility for teaching him what she liked. They successfully expanded their lovemaking, and in time they found satisfaction together.

OTHER PROBLEMS

Vaginismus

Vaginismus is a sexual difficulty that involves an involuntary spasm of the vaginal entrance, making intercourse painful for a woman. This is a fairly rare dysfunction, affecting an estimated 2 percent of women. Vaginismus can make a pelvic examination difficult.

The American Psychiatric Association defines vaginismus as "recurrent or persistent involuntary spasm of the musculature of the lower third of the vagina that interferes with sexual intercourse." Because so much emphasis is placed on coitus, this disorder can cause great concern and anxiety for a couple.

The causes include unconscious fear or guilt, traumatic sexual assaults, painful intercourse, or even a traumatic pelvic examination. Treatment usually starts with exercises for relaxation and self-awareness.

Dyspareunia

Painful intercourse is much more common among women than men and can have a dampening effect on arousal. Inadequate lubrication, poor stimulation, or conflicts in a relationship can cause this disorder. It also could be a matter of insufficient hormones to produce lubrication. Using lubricating jelly can help, but it's important to find the source of the pain to solve the problem.

The pain could be centered at the entrance to the vagina, or the discomfort could involve the clitoral glans. There are many gynecological problems that can produce significant pelvic pain, including endometriosis. This is a condition in which endometrial tissue adheres to other organs of the abdominal cavity, eventually restricting movement of internal organs, and resulting in pain during intercourse. There also are psychological causes, particularly strained relationships, but no matter what the cause, there is excellent treatment for this condition.

Faking Orgasms

Pretending to have an orgasm is a common practice that can evolve into a vicious cycle. One study estimates that nearly 66 percent of women and 33 percent of men have faked an orgasm at one time. The usual reason is a conscious effort not to disappoint a partner, which often results in continued deception to avoid exposure. This pattern can be extremely difficult to break.

Dealing with Male Impotence

- THE PRICE WOMEN PAY
- THE SIGNIFICANT ROLE OF WOMEN

All of us like to watch people while we're waiting in line or strolling through a busy shopping mall. But I have become so intrigued by the subject of sexual dysfunction that I find myself running numbers in my head when I'm in a crowd. *How many of these men are impotent?* I ask myself. Then I think about the women with them. *How are they coping?* I wonder as I look around me.

The discovery that there are millions of impotent men in the United States has caused us to contemplate one of the sadder aspects of our society. And when that eye-opening fact is compounded by the realization that millions of their partners are affected, too, you begin to comprehend the depth of the problem.

My practice now spans three generations of women, so you can appreciate my special affinity for the female side of the foregoing equation. After thousands of confidential conversations and having witnessed the ups and downs of many relationships, I recognize that male impotence takes a significant toll on women. But I also have reached the conclusion that because of their strengths and uniqueness, women can play a critical role in addressing the problem.

THE PRICE WOMEN PAY

It's an old story. The ardent suitor gradually becomes inattentive after settling into the routine of marriage. Many couples reach some accommodation in these cases, and their uninspired love lives remain a very private matter.

For one of my patients, the waning interest of her successful, athletic husband was excruciatingly painful. His legal practice was booming, but his attractive young wife was suddenly taking extreme measures to rekindle romance in their marriage. She had an operation for breast implants, and she even resorted to liposuction to solve a "problem" that was invisible to me.

I had been puzzled by her behavior, of course. But when she finally confided in me, describing how ugly and unappealing she felt, how her once-amorous husband had become chilly in bed, I became suspicious. Fortunately, we were dealing with a man who was willing to consider that *he* had a problem.

After some counseling and a referral to an internist, it was discovered that his testosterone level was that of a young boy. No wonder he was having problems, and what a shame his wife had responded so drastically. Testosterone treatments have done wonders for his libido, and their relationship prospers to this day, although her recovery was a lengthy process.

A woman's reaction to her partner's problem can be complex, running the gamut from extreme frustration to deep concern, to relief that she doesn't have to have sex anymore. Or she may become convinced that she is the cause of the impotence and wonder if it would be different for him with someone else. If any of these feelings sound familiar, please understand that such emotions are normal, and that you are not alone in feeling the way you do.

Typically, the first response is concern that something has hurt the relationship, which can lead to anger and frustration with a husband or partner, especially if a communication problem already exists. But a woman can imagine that she is unattractive or that her partner doesn't love her anymore and is having an affair. Some women are so disturbed that they worry about being abandoned.

Now that it is widely known that erectile dysfunction usually has a physical basis, it's easy to jump to the conclusion that the man you love is ill as well as impotent. Many women worry so much about the possibility of a dangerous health problem that they make their sexual difficulties even worse. Another response of many women is to give up, turning off their own desires, and accepting life without sex. Unfortunately, this usually leads to deep feelings of rejection and depression.

Despite how powerful all of these emotions can be, many women are reluctant to act, and many couples avoid the issue entirely. You probably know people like this, the ones who end up in divorce court or who endure years of emptiness together. But the truth is nobody should suffer needlessly when impotence is the issue. There are too many answers, too many physical and emotional solutions available to those who are willing to seek them.

THE SIGNIFICANT ROLE OF WOMEN

Although a large number of people will disagree with me, I don't believe it's a woman's duty to be the nurturer in a relationship. And I certainly don't share the belief that women exist to serve their mates in a submissive role. But I do contend that women should be aggressive in dealing with male impotence *for their own sake*.

All of us need to be loved in ways that have little to do with a penis being inserted into a vagina. Being held, for example, is one of the most important behaviors for emotional well-being from childhood to old age for both sexes. When couples withdraw from such basic behavior, much of the "glue" that keeps them together is lost.

Good sex is *not* about a man's erection or a woman having an orgasm. Don't get me wrong, those orgasms and erections are definitely a plus. But good sex also is about intimacy, closeness, trust, and having someone with whom you feel safe. Women need to convey this thought to partners having erection difficulties, because a man's first reaction is to withdraw affection rather than risk embarrassment.

If you and your husband are going to have a lasting and hopefully passionate relationship, it will require dedication and persistence. In the end, your investment of time and energy might produce a closer, more satisfying relationship. But be prepared to listen and possibly swallow your pride and acknowledge that your spouse has been right all along about something.

If you really love him, you will need to meet him halfway and put aside your desires temporarily to focus on his needs. And if there has been criticism, anger, and sarcasm in your relationship, these issues have to be addressed and resolved before proceeding with improving sexual involvement. Couples can become entrenched in their positions and unwilling to compromise when there is constant conflict or silent anger without resolution.

You Need to Know

There is no condition that is more humiliating or devastating to a man than impotence.

The ability to function sexually is linked to how a man sees himself and his role in the world.

In most cultures, a huge amount of the male's self-esteem is defined by his erection. Serious depression can be the result of failure to produce one.

Some men withdraw from any sexual activity for fear of failure to achieve an erection. Such acute anxiety virtually ensures erection problems.

A young couple came to Connie Engels on the verge of divorce. They had been married for four years with an adequate sex life until the end of the second year when the husband started experiencing occasional impotence. The wife, who had an overbearing personality, had become very frustrated and was quite vocal in expressing her displeasure.

The husband had pulled back and had lost his sexual desire, eventually admitting that he felt inadequate—a complete failure. When he was a child his mother had told him that he wasn't good enough and was a loser just like his father, who had left her. Now he was hearing a similar message from his wife, and he couldn't disagree.

The husband was deeply depressed when he began therapy, and his wife was openly critical and increasingly angry with him. They were making a lot of mistakes with each other, but at least they had the sense to seek help. Initially, the therapy centered on communication, teaching them how to understand the emotions that were causing their problems, and how to talk about them. The next phase included a prescription for Viagra to help with his periods of impotence, which had a lot to do with emotional issues.

Finally, time was devoted to helping them expand their sexual repertoire and dealing with the wife's unrealistic expectations. But once their displeasure with each other had subsided, and the focus was placed on their sexual problems, they learned to accept their limitations and still give pleasure to each other.

Some women handle male impotence poorly, as in the case we just cited, and the disintegration of a marriage often is the result. But my years of experience with female patients and the education I have received from Ms. Engels have convinced me that women hold the key to saving relationships marred by impotence.

Who is more health conscious? Who sees a doctor more often? Women, of course. As we've said, a man's immediate reaction to erectile dysfunction usually is to clam up and to avoid any behavior that indicates sex is in the offing. So the answer has to be the female partner acting not only to help her mate but also *for her own benefit.*

The easy advice is to tell you to concentrate on communication, but dealing with an impotent man requires more than expressing sympathy and understanding. A woman in this situation who is willing to educate herself is a step ahead, and I am going to recommend some excellent reading material (see page 67). But I also want to make some suggestions that should enable you to *talk* constructively about sex with your partner.

▓ Be willing to listen. Successful communication should be two-sided, but being an *active* listener is the secret. Don't be one of those people who drifts into another world during a conversation. Ask questions, make brief comments, show by your body language that you are interested.

▓ Try paraphrasing what your partner is telling you. Listen to what is being said then summarize the message. If it isn't clear the first time, listen to the message again using different words, then summarize. The paraphrasing technique works best if both of you do it, but one good listener is better than none.

▓ Your eyes are wonderful for expressing feelings. Maintain eye contact during a conversation, which gives a clear signal that you are listening carefully. This is a form of feedback that confirms to your partner that the message is being received.

Discuss in depth with your partner your desires and your fears. Be willing to negotiate your differences and identify the sexual behaviors you each want or are willing to experiment with. Develop a contract. Many couples find it difficult to talk openly about sex. They feel embarrassed about asking for what they want, and they feel shy about their bodies. Some people also feel guilty about their ideas and wishes regarding sex, especially those who were brought up in strict homes where such thoughts were not addressed.

Here are some topics many couples find difficult to discuss:

▓ Erection problems

▓ Orgasmic problems

▓ Partner's hygiene

▓ Oral sex or variety

▓ Use of vibrators

▓ Sexual fantasies

A woman dealing with an impotent man often needs more than self-help, and I believe medical intervention is a must because of the probability that there is a physical problem involved. But I must warn you that too many doctors don't know any more than you do about sex. They may be brilliant in their fields, but they enter practice with very little if any sex education.

Ms. Engels has told me about a client who as a young woman had gone to her family doctor for help because she couldn't have an orgasm. He told her that she obviously was frigid and that there was no treatment. Twenty years later, still victimized by the original diagnosis, she finally received the needed therapy. My recommendation to physicians is that they include a qualified sex therapist as a treatment option, and my advice to you is to do the same.

Don't put up with ignorance and misinformation. If both of you want a sexual relationship that includes intercourse, visit your doctor or go directly to a sex therapist. Women whose husbands refuse to make that move should go for it alone. Get some help!

Words of Wisdom

■ EXPLODING MYTHS
■ WHEN TO SEE A SEX THERAPIST

A very proper, reserved newlywed came to me as a last resort and explained the pain she was suffering during intercourse. She had been brought up by very protective parents, had not had sex before marriage, and was convinced divorce was imminent.

An examination revealed enlarged labia minora that interfered with entry of the penis, eliminating any possibility of enjoyable sex. She had no idea that this was abnormal until our discussion. A surgical procedure quickly solved her problem, but I was once again struck by how critical it is for women to talk to their doctors to find out what is normal and what is not.

- It's very important to develop a close relationship with your doctor, which can be hard to do considering current trends in modern medicine. You need to be able to confide in him and reach solutions together. Unless the cost is prohibitive, don't let higher insurance premiums affect a good doctor-patient relationship.

- I'm going to say it again. By all means have a Pap smear every year. If all women would do this we could come close to eradicating cancer of the cervix. This test and an annual checkup should be musts.

- Learn how to inspect your breasts and do it often. Don't wait for a scheduled checkup if you spot any abnormalities. Doing this on a daily basis could save your life.

Many women have been caught in the painful chain of events that hurt the relationship of a woman I know. It began when her longtime boyfriend came home drunk one night, insisting on having sex. When she finally gave in, he couldn't produce an erection. The next time, in a more sober, tender situation, he remembered his previous failure, which resulted in another "catastrophe." Then, always fearful of another domino falling, his anxiety produced even more failures. He was "working" at making an erection happen and was ignoring stimulation that usually had produced arousal.

Psychological problems, relationship skills, and misinformation are at the core of many of our sexual difficulties. All of us hope for passion and intimacy with our mates, but most couples have trouble sustaining it for these reasons. When something happens to interrupt our sexual functioning, regardless of the cause, it is very easy to slip into an avoidance pattern, which can occur gradually or happen very quickly. The next step is not to even think about sex, and when intimacy is gone, other areas of a relationship are affected, too.

So what should you do? First, decide to take responsibility for your end of the problem. Then ask yourself some important questions. Are you willing to put your frustration, hurt, and anger aside? Are you willing to risk being vulnerable again? Are you willing to stretch yourself and be willing to learn and grow? If all of the answers are "yes," ask your partner to make a similar decision.

Now you're ready to start a self-help program together. Buy a book to guide you through the process, and Ms. Engels recommends *7 Weeks to Better Sex* by Domeena Renshaw, M.D. Your goal is to return to normal functioning sexually, to reestablish closeness, and in the process learn ways that add spice to your lovemaking.

- Follow the book closely and don't skip any of the exercises. You will learn about sexual expression and how the body actually works when you are turned on sexually. All of us are ignorant to some degree in this area, and we need to understand how our genitals work.

- Talk to each other about family histories and the sexual beliefs you were taught. Because all of us have trouble discussing sex, these exercises offer a starting point for getting the subject out in the open.

- Decide to have a moratorium and put the past behind you, agreeing to relax with each other. This can be difficult, especially if the problem has persisted for some time, and hard feelings have accumulated.

- The next step requires you to communicate, relax, have fun, and be creative. Try the sensual exercises suggested in your self-help book. Techniques will be explained that should help you communicate better and enjoy each other. Then experiment with more creative ways of lovemaking.

Many people shrink from allowing themselves to be passionate because they fear losing control, worry about scaring their partners, or are concerned that they will be ridiculed. It's very important to face the fear of passion and be willing to take the risk. Enjoy your sexuality. Allow yourself to be turned on. Share with your partner how you want to be touched and be willing to experiment.

EXPLODING MYTHS

- A most unfortunate misconception is that men have an infallible instinct about what exactly a woman wants sexually. The truth is that no woman can know what type of stimulation she will respond to at any specific time.

- Another myth is that as men age they will lose their ability to have an erection. With age it does take longer to achieve an erection, but if there is general good health and no psychological problems, men can continue to attain erections into and beyond their eighties.

- Many believe that women after menopause have little interest in continuing to have sex. In fact, women have the ability for sexual expression even though there may be some physiological changes in their bodies. Most of them maintain a high level of interest in touching, closeness, and sexual activity with their partners.

- Ingrained in our Western heritage is the concept that reproduction is the only legitimate reason to have sex. This perpetuates the belief that sex is synonymous with coitus and places great expectations and pressure on couples during intercourse. This way of thinking also devalues sensual acts that have nothing to do with coitus.

Too many women tend to minimize their important role in helping a husband who is having sexual difficulties, seeing it as "his" problem. He needs you, and it probably is up to you to keep your romance alive. Have dinner in a romantic place, plan an evening of entertainment, hold his hand, and make sure he knows you love him.

Barbara, a patient of mine, is a housewife, mother of three, and one of those steady, calm people who seldom shows emotion. We had become close over the years, so I had a ringside seat for the battle to save her marriage.

Her husband was caught in a job he hated, working long hours, and feeling like he was trapped in a bad situation that was getting worse.

They loved each other, but he was so angry and unhappy at work that it was spilling over into his life at home. The marriage was in trouble.

Barbara didn't withdraw and cry over the tension and unhappiness inflicted on her by a husband who was rapidly becoming a stranger. Instead, she consciously became aggressive, wore fresh makeup, got out of her jeans and into a dress or skirt in the evening, went to her hairdresser more often, and splurged on the first manicures of her life. She delivered embraces and tender touches even when they weren't warmly received. More than that, she went out of her way to talk lovingly about their good times together, and she spoke boldly about changing jobs and her willingness to move to another city if necessary.

After witnessing a gradual but healthy transformation in their lives, I asked Barbara what had motivated her, what had driven her to act so decisively other than love for her family.

"We loved each other, and I didn't want to lose that," she told me. "But there was something else. I enjoy sex, and I really missed that part of my life. I wanted it back before not having it became a habit. When you're in a bad mood, it's cold in the bedroom. I decided to be pushy, to go all out for my kids, my husband, but mostly for me."

Others don't react so well in a tough situation like this, so I'm delighted to pass along Barbara's story to patients who tend to retreat along with their husbands when serious sexual problems arise.

WHEN TO SEE A SEX THERAPIST

Physicians and psychotherapists often refer patients to a certified sex therapist as part of a comprehensive treatment plan. This can be particularly helpful for a couple coping with an impotence problem. There often are many emotional, social, or psychological issues in addition to the physical causes of the problem. Here are some questions to consider in helping you decide whether you can benefit from sex therapy. If any of these factors applies to your situation, then approaching a sex therapist is something you should consider.

- Is your relationship with your partner angry and full of conflict? Has either one of you withdrawn to the point where communication is difficult if not impossible?

- Are you or your partner tense about sex? Does either of you have negative feelings about sex?

- Was either one of you sexually abused as a child?

- Does either one of you have a diminished sex drive?

- Does either one of you have another sexual dysfunction that is affecting the relationship?

- Is either one of you uncomfortable touching your partner's genitals?

- Does either of you have obsessive sexual urges?

- If your husband is impotent, have you continued noncoital sexual activity to the point of orgasm? Or does either of you lack the skills to do so?

- Do you lack the skills to express nonsexual affection toward each other?

- Are both of you nervous about discussing your sex life? Do you have difficulty sharing how you want to be more creative and have more fun with each other?

If you would like to explore these issues with a certified sex therapist, contact AASECT, the American Association of Sex Educators, Counselors, and Therapists. This is the premier professional organization that certifies and credentials sexual health practitioners. AASECT certification indicates that the therapist has had rigorous academic training and supervised experience in this field.

If you reside in the Dallas area, I recommend Connie Engels, LMSW-ACP, the certified sex therapist who has made a major contribution to this book project. For a list of certified sex therapists in your state, write AASECT at P.O. Box 238, Mt. Vernon, IA 52314–0238. Be sure to include a self-addressed, stamped, business-size envelope. You also may visit AASECT's Web site at www.aasect.org.

RECOMMENDED READING

Our Sexuality, Sixth Edition, Robert Crooks, Karla Baur, Brooks/Cole, Pacific Grove, Ore., 1996.

Becoming Orgasmic, Julie Heiman, Ph.D., and Joseph Loppiccolo, Ph.D., Fireside Book published by Simon & Schuster.

7 Weeks to Better Sex, Domeena Renshaw, M.D., Dell Publishing.

Hot Monogamy, Patricia Love and Jo Robinson, a Plume Book, Penguin Group.

More Than Good Sex, Daniel Beever, M.S., Asian Publishing.

Passionate Marriage, David Schnarch, Ph.D., Harry Holt & Co.

For Yourself: The Fulfillment of Female Sexuality, Lonnie Barbach, Ph.D., a Signet Book, Penguin Group.

Sex for One, Betty Dodson, Ph.D.

The Soul of Sex, Thomas Moore, Harper Collins Publishers.

Joy of Sex, Alex Comfort, M.D., D.S.C., Mitchell Beazley Publishers.

RECOMMENDED VIEWING

The Better Sex Video Series, Dr. Judith Seifer, AASECT-certified sex therapist, host. Sinclair Distribution Company.

The Couples Guide to Great Sex Over 40, Culley Carson, M.D.; Diana Wiley, M.A., hosts.

Part III

THE CAUSES
OF MALE
IMPOTENCE

The Causes of
Male Impotence

- HOW THE PENIS WORKS
- PHYSICAL FACTORS
- EMOTIONAL FACTORS

I have visions of Sigmund Freud rolling restlessly in his grave when I consider how far we've come in understanding the causes of male impotence since his heyday. Amazing, isn't it, that most of us, including the famous Dr. F, blamed psychological malfunctions almost until the end of the twentieth century. And I confess that the medical profession shoulders a great deal of responsibility for the delay in discovering that the problem isn't solely a matter of the mind.

Let me give you three revealing examples that portray dramatically how we have leaped forward in our understanding of what has caused an epidemic of impotence around the world.

Do you remember the 1969 bestseller *Everything You Always Wanted to Know About Sex but Were Afraid to Ask*? America might have been experiencing a sexual revolution at the time, but most of us were virtually oblivious to the actual causes of sexual dysfunction, especially male impotence. Then along came this book by David Reuben, M.D., which opened many eyes. "There is convincing evidence that the source of male potency is in the brain," wrote Reuben.[19] He stated that about 5 percent of all impotence had a physical basis, but he said that only psychiatry and hypnosis offered potential cures for the problem.

Now move forward twenty years to *The Columbia University College of Physicians and Surgeons Complete Home Medical Guide*, which stated in discussing impotence, "In some men, the problem is caused by a disease, such as diabetes, or the result of prostate and other surgery. More often, however, the problem is psychological rather than physiological."[20] Now there's a *hint* of progress.

Finally, just three years later, *The Johns Hopkins Medical Handbook* provided evidence of a significant change on the part of the medical establishment in its understanding of the problem. After noting that only a decade earlier more than 90 percent of all male impotence cases were blamed on emotional causes, it said, "During the past ten years . . . doctors have come to believe that at least half and perhaps as many as three quarters of all cases have a physiological basis as well."[21]

That's a leap forward, but the pace of enlightenment is almost breathtaking when you realize that we now know there are physical reasons for as much as 95 percent of erectile dysfunction. Diabetes, smoking, alcohol, and illegal drugs are among the leading causes. But there are other culprits. Poor dietary habits, lack of exercise, vascular and nerve damage, prostate cancer, and prescription drugs, which can be very dangerous, too. And evidence is accumulating that even such activities as long-distance bicycling are hazardous to vulnerable areas of the bodies of men and women.

I don't mean to infer that there are no psychological factors contributing to male impotence. Experts estimate that psychological problems are involved in up to 20 percent of all cases.[22] Those symptoms, however, often are a secondary response to a physical problem.

The stress a couple feels when dealing with impotence, no matter what the cause, can be debilitating and require therapy. Even renewed sexual activity brought on by any of the remedies, including Viagra, can trigger or renew serious emotional problems. Illness, anxiety, low self-esteem, guilt, exhaustion, depression, or even simply being a little nervous with a new partner also can have a detrimental effect.

Jim is a personal friend of mine whose bout with impotence is a perfect example of both psychological and physical factors coming into play. His case also reminds us not only of how vulnerable human beings can be but also the unwanted effects of some prescription drugs.

First of all, Jim suffered two blows in a short period of time. His long marriage ended in an amicable but distressing divorce. Then, just months after the divorce was final, he underwent surgery for a brain tumor, which fortunately turned out to be benign.

Soon after that, Jim became involved in a warm relationship with his present wife, but he was startled to find that he couldn't produce much of an erection with his attractive new friend. Both of them were very patient although increasingly frustrated, agreeing that anxiety caused by a new partner so soon after divorce and subsequent brain surgery explained the problem.

But Jim's new love interest, Mary, made an important discovery. She told her best friend about Jim's problem. The friend, in turn, made an interesting connection. *Her* husband had taken the prescription drug Dilantin after surgery and was counseled by his doctor that the anticonvulsant could cause temporary impotence. It did—the effects lasting as long as he took the pills.

Mary's friend remembered Jim's recent operation, and the happy ending is pretty obvious. Jim, who indeed was taking Dilantin, talked to his doctor who finally explained the side effects, and as soon as it was safe, he took Jim off the drug. Several years and one child later, Jim can smile while reluctantly admitting that impotence actually had sapped him of his self-confidence and had almost ruined a precious relationship. I love happy endings, but Jim's story is a strong reminder that all of us—doctors and patients—must be alert to the many potential pitfalls when dealing with impotence.

With that in mind, let's examine the results of our research into the causes of male impotence. The object of this effort is to arm you with the very latest information available on the leading reasons for an affliction that has held mankind in its grip for too long, mostly because of our ignorance. Let's begin with the basics.

HOW THE PENIS WORKS

Erectile dysfunction sounds awful, but if you really want to understand the meaning of the term, you need to examine the mechanics of the male sex organ—the penis.

Basically, the penis is composed of spongy tissue and includes two cylinders called the corpora cavernosa. The cylinders are located on each side of the urethra, and they run the length of the penis. When

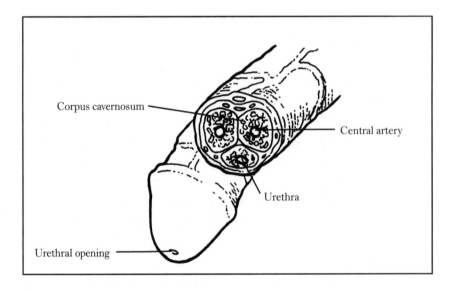

Penis

they are engorged with blood, they become enlarged and create an erection. A fully erect penis contains about eight times as much blood as a nonerect penis.

The whole process begins not in the penis but in the brain. First the man is stimulated—whether visually, physically, or even by a smell or a memory. Then his brain sends the message to his penis through both the autonomic nervous system and the central nervous system.

Once that message is relayed, a substance called nitric oxide is produced in the penis. The nitric oxide initiates the production of another chemical called cGMP, which stands for cyclic guanosine monophosphate. In turn, the cGMP causes the smooth-muscle tissue in the penis to relax. This lets the blood flow into the two corpora cavernosa, which are made up of spongy tissue encased in fibrous tissue. The blood fills up all the tiny spaces in the cylinders. Once that is done, the penis has expanded significantly in both length and girth. *That* is an erection.

When the corpora cavernosa are filled with blood, and the muscle tissue cannot expand any further, the tissue presses up against the veins that normally carry blood away from the penis. This traps the blood within the penis and keeps it erect until the man either ejaculates or otherwise loses his erection. Then the blood is released from the penis, and it flows back toward his heart—and the penis loses its rigidity.

The ejaculatory fluid comes from the testicles, the seminal vesicles, and the prostate gland. It carries sperm from the testicles, and as it starts to build up in the urethra, an orgasm is inevitable—it can't be stopped. When the pelvic muscles and the urethra start to contract, pushing the fluid out of the penis, this causes the physical sensations of the orgasm. During this phase, which is called "resolution," the nitric oxide that has carried the nerve impulse to relax the smooth-muscle tissue is destroyed. And that's how the erection subsides.

Some men have orgasms without an ejaculation. They might have a condition called retrograde ejaculation, or their prostate might have been removed surgically, which would mean an absence of ejaculatory fluid. The prostate is located at the base of the urethra and secretes a liquid that is a major component of the ejaculatory fluid. The key to the buildup of an erection is the nitric oxide, and then the key to the erection subsiding is the subsequent lack of nitric oxide.

When a penis is working properly, an unobstructed flow of blood produces an erection. It's that simple. Now, let's look at what can go wrong.

Physical Factors

- DIABETES
- SMOKING
- ALCOHOL
- ILLEGAL DRUGS
- LEGAL DRUGS
- PROSTATE CANCER
- VASCULAR PROBLEMS
- OTHER FACTORS

DIABETES

Diabetes is by far the most common cause of male impotence, and the evidence is rather startling. According to the American Diabetes Association, the disease by itself accounts for more than 30 percent of all impotence among men. In the bigger picture, vascular disease, of which diabetes is a major contributor, accounts for 40 percent of the known cases.

Placing those percentages in proper perspective is the knowledge that there are 14 million people with diabetes in this country. Another 5 million Americans probably have diabetes but don't know it, and there are five hundred thousand new cases diagnosed each year.[23]

Among diabetic men aged twenty to twenty-nine, 9 percent are believed to be impotent. More than 50 percent of diabetic men older than fifty probably are impotent. For men with diabetes over the age of seventy, 95 percent suffer erectile dysfunction.[24] The effect of the disease on a woman's sexuality can be just as disastrous, although there is far more information available on men. Problems for women include vaginitis, decreased sexual desire, decreased vaginal lubrication, and failure to or increased time to reach orgasm.

Anything that cuts such an unhealthy swath through our society deserves closer scrutiny. Let's start with adult-onset diabetes, which is a very serious disease. If it's not managed properly through diet, exercise, and possibly medication, it can be just as life-threatening as unmanaged juvenile diabetes. So it's crucial for people to pay attention and to report any suspicious problems to their doctors.

The symptoms of adult-onset diabetes, which is now called Type 2, are the same as for juvenile-onset diabetes, which is now called Type 1. But in the case of Type 2, it's too easy to dismiss the symptoms merely as a sign of getting older.

Many of us notice that as the years pass, we might lose a few pounds or will have to get up frequently during the night to urinate. But if these symptoms become particularly bothersome, especially if you notice that you're hungry or thirsty all the time, then it's time to call the doctor. If it turns out that you *do* have adult-onset diabetes, odds are favorable that it can be managed without insulin if you get an early diagnosis.

Other signs to watch for include extreme fatigue, slow healing of sores and infections, numbness or tingling in hands or feet, and blurred vision. It's very important not to ignore any symptoms because Type 2, or adult-onset diabetes, is so very common. According to some estimates as many as 90 to 95 percent of all diabetes is Type 2.

No one should assume that adult-onset diabetes is less serious than juvenile-onset diabetes. Even though the mechanism for adult-onset diabetes is a little different from juvenile diabetes, it can be just as devastating. In both cases, the body's blood sugar levels become impossible to control without some sort of treatment. With juvenile diabetes, the patient might be required to inject insulin for the rest of his life. With adult-onset diabetes he might be able to manage his blood sugar by making lifestyle changes. If he does need drug therapy, there are some oral medications that can be used instead of insulin injections. It depends on several factors, including the severity of the condition.

With juvenile diabetes, the pancreas simply stops manufacturing insulin—which is the hormone that regulates blood sugar levels. With adult-onset diabetes, this is a gradual process. Usually the pancreas continues to manufacture insulin, but it's just not enough. Either way, if the disease is not managed properly, it can cause nerve damage and vascular damage—and that often will lead to impotence.

The way this happens is that in a diabetic, the body's inability to metabolize glucose can lead to arteriosclerosis or hardening of the arteries. This is bad enough in terms of both general health and sexual health. But on top of that, the diminished vascular capability will, in turn, interfere with the blood supply to the nerves. This can cause some serious damage to the central nervous system and the autonomic nervous system. I'm sure you're aware that diabetics are more prone to foot problems, for example, and sometimes even have their feet amputated. If the blood supply to the extremities is cut off, that's what can happen. And, as we have learned, the penis also is vitally affected by blood supply.

An unmanaged case of diabetes can lead not only to impotence but also to cardiovascular problems and other conditions that can, in turn, also lead to impotence. For example, arteriosclerosis, or hardening of the arteries, can lead to hypertension or high blood pressure, which can cause the heart to be overstressed. And those blood-pressure medications can wreak havoc in terms of impotence.

Diet and exercise can help diabetics manage their illness and can greatly improve everyone's cardiovascular fitness. The more you exercise the more sensitive your body's cells become to insulin. Exercise also develops your muscles so that they use up more blood sugar. But the reality is that people do suffer diabetes, heart disease, cancer, and other debilitating diseases despite their best efforts. And our arteries do harden as we age. So it's important to protect ourselves as best we can and to manage these health conditions when we do get them.

You Need to Know

Heredity—If one or both of your parents have diabetes, you are at tremendous risk of developing it yourself.

Race—It is not known why, but African-Americans have twice the risk of developing diabetes as Caucasians, and diabetes also is more common in Hispanics.

Sex—Diabetes is more common in women than in men.

Age—The risk of developing diabetes increases with age.

Cost—The total cost of diabetes and its complications is enormous and is estimated to exceed $20 billion a year.[25]

SMOKING

Amazement swept across the craggy features of Mike Wallace, tough, savvy star of CBS's *60 Minutes*. You wouldn't expect an old pro like Wallace to respond excitedly to any kind of news, but what he was hearing about smoking and impotence obviously was hitting home. I suspect Mike has puffed a cigarette or two in his time.[26]

Here are the key points made in Wallace's *60 Minutes* episode:

■ The aptly named Dr. Randolph Smoak Jr. of the American Medical Association stated flatly that smoking, by itself, is enough to cause impotence.

■ Smokers are twice as likely to have sexual dysfunction. Studies in France, Sweden, South Africa, and the United States have found a far greater percentage of smokers over nonsmokers among impotent patients.

■ Living with a smoker is hazardous to your sex life, too. A study by the New England Research Institute shows that secondhand exposure to smoke at home can double the chances of impotence.

■ Not all smokers will become impotent, but half of all men over forty have problems, and if you smoke you are twice as likely to be one of them.

■ Viagra is not as effective for smokers as it is for nonsmokers because tobacco use decreases the responsiveness of blood vessels, and Viagra depends on that responsiveness to function properly.

■ Thailand became the first country in the world to add to its cigarette warning label, "Smoking causes impotence."

"Why in the world didn't I know about this?" Wallace finally asked one of his guests after hearing a flood of evidence. Then he answered his own question by noting that the "Viagra revolution" has just now put the word "penis" in the news and that there suddenly is a growing awareness of the impotence problem worldwide. "Smoking can kill your sex life," concluded the newly informed Wallace.

The medical profession and other experts have been aware of the danger smoking poses to our sexuality for years. But the general public sometimes needs a jolt from another source before it fully understands the consequences of a bad habit. The *60 Minutes* program hopefully was a wake-up call to many smokers who have been oblivious to the sexual consequences of their bad habit. And when you realize that 25 million men, 23 million women, and more than 4 million teenagers smoke in the United States, there's a lot of waking up to do.

As far as I'm concerned, smoking is one of the worst things men and women can do to themselves. Not only does it cause lung cancer, emphysema, and other diseases, it also badly damages the cardiovascular system. In the case of men, it can lead to a decrease in sperm production, deformed sperm that are less mobile, and decreased blood flow to the penis. Look at it this way—smoking affects the penis in the same way that it does the heart.

Here's what happens: Smoking causes considerable vascular constriction and hardening, which can lead to heart attacks, heart disease, stroke—*and impotence*. The arteries in the penis are incredibly small—only a millimeter or two in diameter. So almost any degree of constriction is going to affect the flow of blood into the penis and therefore impede a man's ability to achieve an erection. For the same reasons, it can hinder arousal and orgasm in women—the fastest-growing group of smokers in the country.

Smoking is extremely damaging to what's known as "vascularization." You may have heard about people who have been ordered to quit smoking before having surgery. That's because good vascularization is essential to healing—the blood has to be able to flow to the part of the body that's being operated on. Diabetics, when undergoing surgery, take much longer to recover because of the vascular damage that the disease can cause if it's not managed properly.

I'm particularly concerned about our prospects for controlling widespread impotence in the future because of smoking trends among teenagers. According to the American Cancer Society, more than three thousand adolescents in the United States smoke their first cigarette *every day*. Compounding the negative health ramifications that stunning number projects is the finding by two Boston physicians—Dr. Alan Greenfield and Dr. Max Rosen—that teenagers who smoke two packs a day could be impotent before they are thirty.

Evidence of the trend is supplied by the University of Michigan Institute for Social Research, which annually surveys national representative samples of high school seniors. Here's what they report:

- The prevalence of daily smoking among high school seniors was 35.1 percent lower in 1987 than in 1977, but was 31.6 percent *higher* in 1997 than in 1987.

- Among female high school seniors, the prevalence of daily smoking was 14.6 percent higher in 1997 than in 1987.

- The only notable reduction in daily smoking among high school seniors was among African-Americans. Their self-reported prevalence decreased 8.9 percent between 1987 and 1997.[27]

If I had a teenage son, I would tell him that the greatest *immediate* risk he could run from smoking is that of impotence. Of course, cancer and heart disease are long-term possibilities, but the threat of impotence will have the most dramatic impact on a male at that age.

I also would be tempted to show him a clever commercial sponsored by the California Health Department. It shows an attractive young man and woman chatting intimately at a bar. As the announcer starts talking about the impotence-related effects of smoking, the camera pans along the bar to a lineup of handsome young men with cigarettes sticking straight out of their mouths, then slowly . . . drooping . . . limply . . . toward the floor. A dazzling young woman on the other side of the bar takes note and swiftly slips away as the commercial ends with the line, "Cigarettes? Still think they are sexy?" (When I watched this clever commercial, I thought of that "dazzling young woman." If she smokes, too, she could have her own problems with sex.)

That may be a clever ploy for threatening smokers, but I certainly don't mean to downplay the brutal fact that one-third of the youngsters who take up smoking today eventually will die of tobacco-related diseases. In all, almost a half-million Americans die every year for the same reason. These are sobering facts, but there is hope for those who overcome the addiction before too much damage has occurred.

Next time you are with someone who is smoking, ask yourself, "Does that person have any idea of what's in store for him or her?" If you are a smoker, my urgent advice is to quit immediately. And if you need help, your doctor can recommend a program that will work for you.

ALCOHOL

The subject of alcohol is less definitive than tobacco. There have been some studies showing that moderate consumption—especially wine—might help promote cardiovascular health. Others have shown that wine contains antioxidants that might help prevent cancer. An issue for women is weighing that potential against other studies that show a possible connection between alcohol and breast cancer.

There's no doubt among credible researchers, though, that alcohol abuse is very dangerous to both men and women. It can lead to impotence as well as other diseases that eventually can be fatal. In the area of sexual performance, many people mistakenly think of alcohol as an aphrodisiac, but in reality it can impair the functioning of the nerves that transmit the message of stimulation from the brain. It also can cause veins to dilate, which in a man can lead to vascular "leakage." And you know what that means: The man won't be able to maintain his erection because the blood will flow back from the penis into the body.

Aside from those short-term effects, long-term alcohol abuse can do permanent damage to our overall well-being as well as our sexual health. Liver disease is almost a certain consequence of chronic alcohol abuse. And a malfunctioning liver can lead to elevated levels of estrogen in relation to testosterone—which in turn can cause a drop in a man's libido.

Incidentally, the same thing can happen to a woman if her estrogen levels are too high—so women should avoid alcohol abuse, and if they're on estrogen therapy, they need to monitor their reactions very closely. So let's review what we learned in Part II about hormones.

Hormones regulate our reproductive systems, the most important being androgens (e.g., testosterone) and estrogens (e.g., estradiol). They are synthesized mainly by the testes and the ovaries respectively and affect our reproductive functions.

Reproductive hormones in men are responsible for sexual maturation, sperm development, and various aspects of sexual behavior. The hormones in women promote development of sexual characteristics, regulate the menstrual cycle, and help maintain pregnancy.

Heavy drinking, especially if it's chronic, interferes with all of these functions. The results can be inadequate production by the testes and ovaries, causing hormonal deficiencies, sexual dysfunction, and infertility.

The bottom line is that alcohol can be toxic to the testes, reducing testosterone levels in men. In premenopausal women, heavy drinking contributes to cessation of menstruation, irregular menstrual cycles, menstrual cycles without ovulation, early menopause, and increased risk of spontaneous abortions.

Beyond these problems, the entire lifestyle of an alcoholic is unhealthy. A heavy drinker is much more likely to be a smoker and much less likely to exercise. An alcoholic or abuser of alcohol is less likely to eat a balanced diet, and this robs the body of the key nutrients that it needs to bolster the immune system and fight off other diseases.

All in all, I think that most people probably can have a drink now and then. But I don't think that nondrinkers should start to consume alcohol because they've heard of potential health benefits. It isn't worth the risk. And alcohol abusers definitely should stop. It's most important to seek help at the first signs of alcoholism—the dangers are too great, and there are no benefits from abusing alcohol.

You Need to Know

Nearly 14 million Americans, including one in every thirteen adults, are alcoholic or abuse alcohol. Several million more have risky drinking habits.

Approximately 53 percent of men and women in this country report that one or more of their close relatives have a drinking problem.

Alcohol abuse problems cost our society approximately $100 billion a year.

Consumption of alcohol can be especially harmful to those with a predisposition to a blood sugar problem. This includes people being treated for diabetes.[28]

ILLEGAL DRUGS

Illegal drugs are far more dangerous than most people realize, especially among Baby Boomers who grew up with more casual attitudes toward street drugs. These drugs can be quite damaging to our sexual health, and they can cause impotence in men as well—even men who stopped using drugs long ago.

I'm not saying that everyone who ever used drugs will end up impotent. After all, there are many other factors involved. But all other things being equal, I'd say the damage done by drugs would be related to how heavily they were used. And so would the degree to which the damage can be reversed.

Probably the most commonly used street drug among the Baby Boom generation was marijuana. Throughout the sixties and seventies, many people assumed that marijuana was safe to use—perhaps even safer than alcohol. And many people still think that. But both marijuana and alcohol actually depress a man's testosterone level, which I think would surprise those who regard these drugs as aphrodisiacs.

Also, there's some research showing that marijuana users have elevated levels of a hormone called prolactin. This is the hormone that induces lactation in women. In men, elevated prolactin levels can actually bring about female characteristics such as enlarged breasts. And it can lead to impotence if there is no treatment. Marijuana use isn't the only thing that can cause elevated prolactin levels, of course. But it is important for men to realize that the condition can be reversed with a drug called Parlodel. So, again, a man should not be hesitant about talking to his doctor.

Cocaine is another drug that was popular with Baby Boomers and the following generation during the eighties. Even well into the nineties, it is estimated that 1.5 million Americans are users of cocaine. Unfortunately, cocaine is one of the most dangerous drugs there is—and I believe it's the most damaging drug of all in terms of sexual health.

The reason cocaine is so dangerous is that it constricts the flow of blood, and it causes nerve damage. This makes cocaine a major threat to our health in many ways—and impotence is just one consequence. I wish that more people knew this—and also that they understood that both the vascular damage and the nerve damage might be permanent. I used to believe that the damage could be reversed if a person stopped using the drug. But since then, I know of cases where the damage has not been reversed, and the man now has to use some sort of impotence therapy.

The truth is that just about any street drug can cause irreparable damage. But, as I said earlier, cocaine is the most destructive. Even heroin, which is so devastating and so addictive, doesn't cause the same degree of vascular or nerve damage as cocaine. But all these drugs are so harmful and so addictive that it is imperative to avoid them altogether.

Ella's case is a perfect example of the destructive force of cocaine on users and their partners. Like a lot of us, she had battled a weight problem for most of her adult life, but she always had kept it somewhat under control. Then one day during a checkup I noticed how awful she looked—much heavier, rather disheveled looking, far from the sharp lady I had known for years.

She had been through a lot, including a hysterectomy that unfortunately had lowered her self-esteem for awhile. And her husband, a hard-driving businessman, had been an even bigger problem. He at one time was a heavy user of cocaine and other drugs, and he had openly conducted affairs with other women. But somehow, with an intervention partly on my part, he had straightened himself out, and Ella had maintained her equilibrium throughout.

But seated across from me on that day several years ago was a defeated woman. She confided that her husband's impotence was sapping all the strength she had exhibited during previous difficult times. Counseling hadn't helped, and she blamed herself for what she thought were his psychological problems. Fortunately, we were beginning to understand that drug use—especially cocaine—could cause nerve damage leading to impotence. I was able to help.

Today, thanks to a good psychotherapist for her and an efficient motorized pump for him, they are once again a loving couple, thriving in every way as they move into their golden years. Their lesson is that drugs can virtually destroy a man's sexual prowess as well as his marriage, but more help is available than most people realize.

LEGAL DRUGS

Impotence also can be a side effect of many prescribed drugs, including cardiovascular medications, antidepressants, tranquilizers, appetite suppressants, gastrointestinal drugs, and certain diuretics.

Beta-blockers, which are prescribed for hypertension, are a big offender—but they're not the only ones.

I've included the accompanying partial list so that you can be prepared when consulting with your doctor. As you scan it, be aware that drugs—both prescription and illegal—account for 25 percent of all cases of impotence, according to the National Institute of Diabetes and Digestive and Kidney Diseases (NIDDK).

Also, people need to realize that over-the-counter medications can cause problems, too. The biggest offenders are antihistamines and sleep medications. Like some of the prescription drugs, they can cause such symptoms as depression or neurotransmitter problems.

I'm not saying that you should avoid medicine because you fear the possibility of impotence. But all of us must be aware that many medications can have negative side effects. Fortunately, impotence usually disappears when the patient stops taking certain drugs. But you should be well informed when taking any kind of medicine for a health problem.

These days, most doctors and pharmacists will mention possible side effects—but just in case, the patient shouldn't be afraid to approach the subject. Also, the patient needs to be aware that there are certain drug combinations that can result in impotence or other side effects—and he should be sure to tell his doctor or pharmacist about other medications he takes. And that includes standard, over-the-counter medicine, not just prescription drugs.

Finally, a man needs to speak up after he starts taking a medication and let the doctor know if he's experiencing impotence. I don't worry much about women talking to their doctors, but men often are reluctant to say anything to theirs in this situation. They know they have to take the medicine, but they mistakenly believe that admitting to impotence is surrendering to a flaw or weakness. Stigmas die hard, don't they?

The good news is that if a prescribed drug is affecting a man's ability to perform sexually, there very well may be an alternative treatment. For example, the doctor may be able to switch the patient from a beta-blocker to a calcium channel blocker to treat hypertension. Of course, the best strategy is to avoid hypertension in the first place.

Drugs That Can Cause Impotence

Cardiovascular, hypertension—Digitalis, Digoxin, Inderal, Lopressor, Sandril

Antianxiety, antidepressant—Diazepam, Elavil, Equanil, Librium, Serax, Stelazine, Tranxene, Valium

Nausea—Combid, Phenergan

Ulcer—Tagamet, Zantac

Prostate tumor—Estrace, Lupron

Diuretic—Diamox, HydroDIURIL

Parkinson's disease—Akineton, Artane, Cogentin, Kemadrin, Pagitane

Miscellaneous—Antabuse, Dilantin, Flagyl, Flexeril, Indocin, Norflex, Sansert

Over-the-counter—Benadryl, Dramamine

Let's face it—so many drugs, both prescription and over-the-counter, have been implicated in sexual impairment that every one of them should be considered guilty of deflating erections or diminishing orgasms until proved innocent.

PROSTATE CANCER

Another condition that becomes more common with age involves prostate problems. A man might notice as he gets older that he needs to urinate more frequently, or that he has difficulty urinating. It's important to see a urologist about these symptoms because there are things a man can do to improve his prostate health. Also, he needs to rule out prostate cancer—which is something people might face as they get older, sometimes as early as their fifties.

Prostate cancer, and especially prostate surgery, definitely can affect a man's sexual health. Instances of prostate cancer are on the rise, possibly because of improved diagnostic techniques. More than 40 percent of all new cancers diagnosed in men are of the prostate, and it's the second-leading cause of cancer death in men. In 1999, it was estimated that 179,300 men would be diagnosed with prostate cancer, and almost 37,000 would die of it.[29]

Don't jump to conclusions, however. A diagnosis of prostate cancer does not mean there is no hope. Nor does it necessarily require surgery. Each case is different. Generally, if a man is older and the tumor looks like it's under control, the doctor will recommend against radical surgery. But with some younger men, surgery is recommended more often. This is not something that a doctor will advise unless it's absolutely necessary. But it is important for the patient to know that there is the potential for nerve damage. In fact, any surgery in that part of the body—prostate, bladder, rectum, anywhere in the pelvic area—does have that potential.

A patient who is about to undergo a radical prostatectomy—which is the complete removal of the prostate—obviously has little choice in the matter. Clearly, the doctor has determined that the surgery is a must. But there is a 70 percent chance that it will cause nerve damage that will result in impotence, especially if the case is more advanced. Some of the newer surgical techniques may reduce that percentage, but the possibility still exists. And, unfortunately, this kind of nerve damage is irreversible—although even here, a pump or an implant can sometimes be effective in sustaining sexual activity.

Most men undergoing a radical prostatectomy will not be able to have an erection for three to twelve months after the operation. Eventually some of them will be able to achieve an erection and others still will have trouble. Following the operation, a man's ability to have an erection is related both to his age and type of surgery that was done. It's important to note, however, that penile sensation and the ability to have an orgasm remain even if the erectile nerves are removed during radical prostatectomy.

You Need to Know

More than eight out of ten men with prostate cancer are over the age of sixty-five.

The malignancy is more common among African-Americans.

The actual cause of prostate cancer remains unknown, although a high-fat diet is suspected. I suggest eating foods high in fiber and low in fat.

Most men treated with radiation therapy become impotent.

The rate of prostate cancer is declining, although next to skin cancer it is the most common diagnosis.

The prostate, about the size of a walnut, is located just below the bladder and in front of the rectum, and the tube that carries urine (urethra) runs through the prostate.

VASCULAR PROBLEMS

Remember, achieving and sustaining an erection depends on the strength of the vascular system to keep the blood in the penis. And we know that for women, their sexual performance also is impacted by how the same system functions.

The arteries that carry blood into the genital area are very narrow. That's one reason for men and women to maintain good cardiovascular health. Hardening of the arteries and the arterial blockage that causes it are both very dangerous to our health. But they also can cause impotence by narrowing those arteries so much that the blood can't flow into the penis or vagina, for example.

The veins that carry the blood away from the penis are larger than the arteries leading in. And those veins need to be blocked in order for the erection to be maintained. Otherwise, the man will be able to achieve an erection but will quickly lose it as the blood leaks away. Or the tissue inside the corpora cavernosa could lose its elasticity and its ability to relax enough to let the blood flow in. When that happens, the tissues don't expand properly, and they don't exert enough pressure to prevent the blood from flowing out of the penis.

This leakage problem happens sometimes in men who suffer hardening of the arteries or arteriosclerosis. Less frequently, radiation therapy near the base of the penis can cause a loss of elasticity. If there's a leak that can be pinpointed, then surgery might correct the leak. But if there is some arteriosclerosis, it's important to realize that the arterial damage is irreversible—and not only that, it's also a sign that overall cardiovascular health is not good.

Nerve Damage

In addition to vascular damage, nerve damage also can result in impotence. Remember, the message of stimulation has to be transmitted from the brain to the penis in order to start the production of nitric oxide. Otherwise, the smooth-muscle tissue in the penis will not relax, allowing the blood to engorge the two cylinders. Also, the nerves have to maintain that message of stimulation from the brain so that the tissue stays engorged and the blood doesn't leak out.

Nerve damage can be caused by many factors. Whether or not we can prevent the damage depends on the cause. For example, diabetes is a big threat to both the cardiovascular system and to the nervous system. Other diseases, like multiple sclerosis and Parkinson's, also can cause impotence through nerve damage.

Surgery, especially prostate surgery, can sever the neurovascular bundles, particularly if the prostate cancer is very advanced, and the tumor is very large. So it's important for a patient, his wife, and his doctor to weigh the pros and cons of surgery, and it's also important for all men to take whatever lifestyle measures they can to help protect against prostate cancer.

OTHER FACTORS

Aside from prostate surgery, there are other factors that can damage the nerves enough to result in impotence, including:

Bicycle Riding

Hard, narrow bicycle seats can cause impotence after prolonged cycling. The problem is created when pressure is put on arteries and nerves in the groin that supply blood and feeling to the genital area in men and women. The first sign of trouble usually is numbness—the same kind of sensation as your foot falling asleep.

Dr. Irwin Goldstein of Boston University is an expert on impotence who has led the way in raising questions about extensive bicycle riding. He maintains that it takes just 11 percent of a man's weight to compress penile arteries onto the conventional bike seat. Over time, he contends, the arteries fail to bounce back, becoming crushed, and causing blockages.

Dr. Goldstein estimates that there are one hundred thousand men who have become impotent because of too much time on bike seats or accidents on the top tubes. He also warns that stationary bikes can be just as tough on the blood supply to the penis.

A 1997 article in *Bicycling* magazine quotes Dr. Goldstein as saying, "Men should never ride bicycles. Riding should be banned and outlawed. It's the most irrational form of exercise I could ever bring to discussion. Fifty percent of the penis is actually inside the body. When a man sits on a bicycle seat he's putting his entire body weight on the arteries that supply the penis. It's a nightmarish situation."[30]

There are a number of other doctors who contend, however, that the health benefits of cycling surpass what they consider an unknown risk. I for one believe that extended riding on a narrow, hard seat can contribute to erectile problems and that all riders, men and women, should be aware of the danger and do something about it.

Some manufacturers have redesigned the bicycle seat to make life for cyclists a little more comfortable and more carefree. A hollowed-out area provides a safe haven for the vulnerable parts of the groin, allowing blood to flow more freely and redistributing body weight away from the bundle of arteries and nerves that can be damaged by more traditional seats.

If you're worried about this, switch to one of the newly designed seats—hollowed out and with gel padding. There also are seats designed specifically for a woman's body because of debilitating problems they experience in the genital area. Meanwhile, here are some simple precautions all cyclists should take:

- Make sure your seat is adjusted properly as far as height and tilt are concerned. Your knee should be slightly bent at the bottom of the pedal stroke, and the seat probably should be angled a few degrees forward.

- Don't allow your pelvis to move from side to side while riding. Be a relaxed, stable rider with little upper-body movement.

- Get off the bike periodically, especially if there is numbness or discomfort.

Peyronie's Disease

One of my patients endured a long period of sexual inactivity because her husband had a badly bent penis. In his situation, an erection was extremely painful, and intercourse was impossible. His penis was damaged in a fall while hiking, but there are other causes of this disorder, including heavy use of alcohol.

The bent penis syndrome, Peyronie's disease, is the result of scar tissue forming along the walls of the erectile chambers of the penis. The scarring, a result of plaque deposits, bends the penis to the side where the scarring is most severe. The problem affects about 1 percent of men in the most vulnerable age group—over forty.[31] It can occur for no obvious reason, and it can eventually disappear. Or it can be the result of trauma, as in the case of my patient's husband.

Often surgery is required to correct the deformity no matter what the cause. And for my patient's husband, a surgical procedure restored the intimacy the couple had been missing for years.

The Workplace

Occupational exposure to toxic chemicals—lead and other heavy metals in particular—also might contribute to impairment of sexual ability.

EMOTIONAL FACTORS

- PERFORMANCE ANXIETY
- STRESS
- LOW LIBIDO
- DEPRESSION

Most couples dealing with impotence, no matter what the cause, have to address important emotional and psychological issues that can't help but affect them. After coping with impotence for some time, many couples find it helpful to seek treatment from a qualified sex therapist or some other professional who can assist them in reconnecting emotionally.

Connie Engels, the certified sex therapist that we introduced earlier, says that emotional problems that couples experience in connection with male impotence usually will fall into three categories:

straightforward problems that are clearly related to the husband's impotence, relationship problems, and serious psychological problems.

The straightforward problems, of course, are the easiest to address. One of the most common, Ms. Engels says, is that if the man is now using a device or an implant, the woman feels that the erection is artificial. In fact, the woman could be in a lot of emotional pain because she believes that she has nothing to do with turning on her husband. In a case like this, a therapist can help the couple explore their feelings, and also to come up with creative ways to include the device in their lovemaking so that they both feel sexy again.

Relationship problems, according to Ms. Engels, require a different approach. Sometimes these types of problems existed before but did not surface until the man became impotent. Also, it's not unusual for a man and woman to build up a lot of hurt and frustration when they've been dealing with impotence for a long time. These unresolved feelings can affect other parts of their relationship, and they can definitely interfere with their sexual desire for each other. They also can affect how the couple deals with other problems in their lives. So it is most important to seek help in resolving these issues.

Serious psychological problems will require an intense effort by both the patient and the therapist. These issues can include serious clinical depression, a childhood history of sexual abuse, compulsive sexual urges—there are many things that can surface during treatment for sexual dysfunction. Ms. Engels tells me that in many of these cases she highly recommends individual therapy.

PERFORMANCE ANXIETY

Even Masters and Johnson, who were so instrumental in establishing the field of sex therapy, maintained that male impotence was largely psychological. They accepted a Freudian-style theory that a grown man's sexual problems stemmed from his childhood, specifically a bad relationship with a female family member. But Masters and John-son did make some important contributions to the study of impo-tence, even though they didn't realize the importance of the physiological causes at that time.

For one thing, they were the first to define "performance anxiety." This is not the same thing as impotence, although some people seem to think it is. A lot of people use the phrase "performance anxiety" for all sorts of things today. In the area of sexual dysfunction, it means that a man's anxiety creates a rush of adrenaline that diminishes the flow of blood to the penis, which interferes with the man's erection. That has happened to most men at one time or another, and it can be considered a temporary form of impotence. But it's not the same thing as the chronic condition that we are discussing here.

It's important to realize, too, that almost all men will experience impotence at some point in their lives, whether it's caused by illness, injury, anxiety, exhaustion, or even just being a little nervous with his partner. And we do have to credit Masters and Johnson with pointing that out. In their clinical trials, they found that these isolated episodes of impotence were no indication of a long-term, chronic condition—and that's a very important point.

Masters and Johnson made another important contribution, which was their discovery of the cultural and social factors that can affect our sexual behavior as adults. For example, many people are raised to believe that certain things are immoral or unacceptable, like birth control, oral sex, or even sex itself. So it's easy to understand why chil-dren who are taught these beliefs might grow up to become sexually dysfunctional adults. Also, Masters and Johnson should be recognized for pointing out the importance of a couple's emotional relationship.

Here's an example of what I mean. As you know, if a man has been impotent for a while, there can be a lot of emotional stress in the mar-riage. Often, even if the husband seeks help for the physical problem that has caused his impotence, couples may have trouble resuming sexual activity with any frequency. That's because of the emotional factors that the couple still has to deal with—and even some psychological factors that may come to the surface because of the man's physical problems.

STRESS

We're all under stress to some extent in our demanding, modern society, but that doesn't mean we become impotent as a result. Sometimes we're just tired or preoccupied. There are so many things that can distract people these days, sometimes for extended periods of time—our kids, our work, our finances, an illness, a family member's illness—the list is almost endless. But there are many ways that people can learn to cope with day-to-day frustrations or even long-term problems—such as regular exercise, eating properly, meditation, or maybe some sessions with a counselor.

The truth is that stress does not actually cause impotence. Stress is certainly a side effect of impotence, and it can make a man and woman even more frustrated. But everyday stress just is not the same thing as the emotional and psychological issues we've been talking about. Overall, I think that stress gets the blame for too much.

Obviously, stress in a marriage almost certainly will cause a loss of sexual desire if the source of the stress is not dealt with. Anger is a common cause of this kind of stress. Even if the two partners love each other and are basically happy in their marriage, they can still be angry enough to inhibit their sexual desire for each other.

When one of my patients expresses angry feelings toward her husband, I try to help her open the lines of communication between the two of them. Failing that, I encourage them to talk to a marriage counselor, a sex therapist, or a psychotherapist. Once the underlying problems are addressed and resolved, and communication improves between the husband and wife, then the sexual problems can be addressed.

Sylvia and Tom are an example of what we're talking about, and they are proof that the mind can be at the heart of problems in our sex lives.

I was privileged to deliver their first child, and they were as thrilled as any couple I have ever seen with a new baby. But, as you might have guessed, there was a complication. The healthy young mother breezed through her postpartum examination about five weeks after delivery and was ready to have sex. But nothing happened. Her nervous husband wouldn't come near her.

There were many excuses—"We'll wake the baby," or "I'm afraid I'll hurt you." The problem had festered for some time when she came in for her annual Pap smear and tearfully told me about the situation. Sylvia's husband, whom I had met several times, was in great shape, had no history of alcohol abuse, drug abuse, or hypertension. So I referred him to Connie Engels.

She quickly got to the root of the problem. Tom was so consumed by his added responsibility and irrational fear of another pregnancy that he had been rendered—in effect—impotent. Time and a big assist from therapy restored the missing element of an otherwise happy marriage. There's no sign of a second child yet, but this case was a reminder that not all sexual difficulties can be attributed to physical factors.

LOW LIBIDO

Something else that's frequently cited these days as detrimental to enjoying sex is "male menopause." Whether such a condition exists is controversial, but there are a lot of things that can interfere with a man's libido. Both men and women can be preoccupied with everything from day-to-day problems to serious threats to their health, or that of their loved ones.

It's true that some men do experience hormone deficiencies as they get older. If a man's testosterone level drops, then his libido certainly will suffer. And there are many physical conditions that can cause a hormone deficiency, as we previously have discussed. Another look at alcoholism provides an example. As you know, many people mistakenly assume that alcohol can "loosen them up"—that it is a sort of aphrodisiac. But the truth is that chronic alcohol abuse can lead to liver disease, which in turn can lead to higher estrogen levels and a decline in libido.

Also, there are many health conditions that can cause a person's sex drive to dwindle. In general, when someone just doesn't feel well, he or she probably will lose interest in sex even if not clinically impotent. Prostate cancer, for example, can make a man tired and irritable, and it can cause premature ejaculation. Or take cardiovascular disease or hypertension—either of these can lead to male impotence, but they also can cause headaches and chest pain and other symptoms that make sexual activity very uncomfortable. All in all, it's wise for everyone to work at staying as healthy as possible.

It is important, though, to make the distinction between a lack of interest, a low libido, and clinical impotence. Simply stated, if a man is impotent, it means that his penis isn't working properly.

DEPRESSION

A significant source of sexual problems is depression, which is so common that it often is called "the common cold of mental health problems." The World Health Organization reports that 340 million people worldwide suffer the disorder, and more than 17 million of them are Americans.[32]

Of particular interest here is the knowledge that loss of libido is a classic symptom of depression, with experts estimating that about 75 percent of clinically depressed individuals report a loss of their sex drive. Compounding the problem is the fact that certain antidepressants are notorious causes of impotence among men and women. Sexual impairment is as high as 50 percent among those who take them.

Depression, which can be difficult to diagnose, has biochemical roots that affect the way nerve cells in the brain work. Unusually high levels of several brain chemicals are found in severely depressed people, which may be inherited and is the reason why depression tends to run in families. However, although researchers are looking for a genetic connection, no "depression gene" has been discovered. And people who have lived happy lives can become seriously depressed, the brain chemistry slipping for no apparent reason.

Psychotherapy is the time-honored treatment. But increasingly the answer to depression is medication, with antidepressants elevating the mood of up to 80 percent of those who use them as directed. There are a number of serotonin reuptake inhibitors available, and all of them are effective. But some work better for different combinations of symptoms than others.

Prozac, Zoloft, and Paxil are the most prescribed antidepressants, and they are believed to cause sexual impairment in up to half of the people using them. There are a number of ways to deal with such side effects, including dose reduction, changing medication, or by taking certain antidotes. Consulting with your doctor if you believe a drug is harming your sex life is the best way to protect yourself from complications.

As you probably know, this is one of the most treatable of all psychological disorders, although it is estimated that only a third of those who suffer serious depression seek treatment. In this section, we have examined quite an array of reasons why impotence is so rampant, but in virtually every case there is help available for those who will ask. Next, we will analyze various methods for restoring dormant sex lives with a broad, sweeping bow to that drug of drugs, *Viagra*.

But first:

You Need to Know

1 One in four women and one in ten men will develop depression in their lifetime. Depression affects one in fifty children under age twelve and one in twenty teenagers.

2 The World Health Organization predicts that by the year 2020, depression will be the greatest burden of ill health to people in the developing world.

3 Depression is estimated to cost $43 billion a year for medication, professional care, and lost workdays.

4 Most depressed people continue to function, with 72 percent of them in the workforce.

5 Deep emotional losses may trigger the biochemical changes that cause depression.

6 Antidepressants are not so addictive, but overdosing can be fatal.

7 The first antidepressants, monoamine oxidase (MAO) inhibitors, were accidentally discovered by researchers trying to develop drugs to combat tuberculosis.[33]

Part IV

TREATING MALE
IMPOTENCE

Treating Male Impotence

- VIAGRA
- TIME-TESTED TREATMENTS
- TAKING THE INITIATIVE

Viagra, Viagra, Viagra, everybody is clamoring for the drug—men who *can't* do it, men who *can* do it but want more, and a growing number of women who want to resuscitate their limp libidos, too. That coveted little pill not only is restoring long-dormant sex lives, it also has produced an enlightening array of other benefits for our suddenly sexier society.

Men, notorious for avoiding doctors, are begging for appointments, finally confronting their impotence, and making some critical discoveries about themselves along the way. There have been many cases where men have agreed to long-delayed checkups just to get a prescription for Viagra, and in the process find that they have a serious health problem. Physicians—and thousands of women—are thrilled that so many men are finally coming out of hiding and making some life-saving discoveries.

Yes, the new wonder drug is highly effective, producing results for approximately 70 percent of those who try it. But that leaves a sizable number of men who get nothing but headaches, flushed faces, and blue-tinted vision when they pop the pill. Those impotence sufferers are finding that there are other ways to bring back sexual pleasure without Viagra—existing treatments that have worked well for many men.

The millions who suffer from sexual dysfunction today have ample reason to hope that their love lives can be rekindled. And Viagra, of course, has been the answer for many of them, but when it doesn't work, there are implants, injections, vacuum pumps, and testosterone patches available that have proved to be just as effective over a longer period of time.

But please don't discount the psychological aspects of impotence. There are specialists in the field of sex therapy who can cushion the impact of renewed sexual activity as well as help people focus on deep-seated emotional problems that hinder them sexually. The mind remains a powerful force even though most impotence can be traced to physical factors.

Viagra

- AN ACCIDENTAL SUCCESS
- HOW VIAGRA WORKS
- THE SAFETY FACTOR
- VIAGRA FOR WOMEN
- OTHER POSSIBILITIES
- WHAT ABOUT THE FUTURE?

So what is this bit of blue that is turning on the world? For one, it's a runaway moneymaker, a booming best-seller beyond anything ever seen in the highly competitive drug industry. For another, it's simple and usually painless to use. But most of all, it works in the majority of cases. Just pop the pill about an hour before intercourse, have some stimulating foreplay, and enjoy!

The Viagra steamroller began in March 1998 with approval by the FDA and was available in pharmacies by mid-April of that year. It was a much-heralded, mind-boggling success from day one, with thirty-six thousand prescriptions written for the drug in only its second week on the market.

Discovered and developed by Pfizer Inc., a research-based pharmaceutical giant with global operations, Viagra sales for the first year were stunning testimony to the fact that millions of men wanted their sex lives back—even at ten bucks a pop. Pfizer reported in January 1999 that its fourth-quarter revenues in 1998 increased 26 percent over the fourth quarter of 1997. (This is a company with reported total sales in 1998 of more than $13.5 billion.)[34]

Sales of Viagra were $236 million for the fourth quarter of 1998 and $788 million for the year. By early 1999, two hundred thousand U.S. physicians had written more than 8 million prescriptions for more than 4 million patients.[35] Viagra is now available in more than forty countries, including the United Kingdom, Germany, France, Italy, Spain, Brazil, Australia, and Japan. The more optimistic forecasters believe the drug is on track to do $1.4 billion in sales in 1999.

While the Viagra craze continues, there has been some slippage in the still-impressive numbers. Within a month of its release, doctors were writing about three hundred thousand prescriptions a week, and worldwide sales reached $411 million for the first quarter. Recent statistics are somewhat sobering. Prescriptions are now running about 170,000 a week, and worldwide sales had dipped to $141 million for the third quarter in 1998[36] before rebounding by the end of the year.

What I see is a natural sorting out of those who actually don't need the drug, those who get nothing out of it, and those who fear the possible side effects. I also understand there are a number of men who simply needed a boost of confidence, which Viagra provides, and now they are able to go it on their own. But beyond all the numbers, I believe Viagra's true legacy has been its ability to lure many men out of hiding who actually have health problems that need attention.

AN ACCIDENTAL SUCCESS

Sildenafil citrate, as Viagra is scientifically labeled, may have produced a bonanza for its producers and a surge of sexual potency for its consumers, but it was a failure in its original role. In fact, it would have been tossed on the trash heap and forgotten if it hadn't been for an accidental discovery.

The drug initially was tested in the 1980s in the United Kingdom as a medication for patients diagnosed with coronary heart disease. It was believed that the drug's demonstrated ability as a smooth-muscle relaxer might open up constricted arteries and help relieve severe angina pains. But sildenafil citrate finally was abandoned because it was found to be virtually useless in its intended role.

Then, almost by chance, researchers made a startling discovery. Patients participating in the test program who also suffered erectile dysfunction were gushing about a wonderful side effect—erections that rivaled the best of their lives. They didn't want to give up the pill, and a wonder drug was born by accident. Yes, the rest is history.

Now, testimonials to the attributes of Viagra are commonplace, and as you might imagine, I'm hearing more stories than most people. Harry, who is a colleague of a friend, also is a published author, so I'm going to let him relate his success with Viagra in his own words . . .

> More than twelve years after my first wife's death, and after I was well into my sixties, I met at a reunion a woman who had been a childhood playmate. We were friends through high school and college but had been out of touch more than forty years. Love ignited for both of us; and although we were separated by almost two thousand miles, we initiated a series of rendezvous and began talking about marriage. Our wedding occurred fourteen months after our reunion; and it was my new wife's wish that sex be deferred until our wedding night.

She had been divorced more than twenty years and had known no post-marital sexual activity whatever. In the years of my widowed state, my own sexual experience had been spasmodic, and I was aware of a slight but steady diminishing of sexual vigor. I had been celibate more than a year before we married, so I was somewhat relieved that our wedding night was a modest sexual success. My wife's first wedding night, when she lost her virginity, was a remembered nightmare, and she had experienced little sexual pleasure in her twenty-year marriage. However, she did not achieve a climax on our wedding night. That did not occur until I swallowed pride and decided to try Viagra.

Our lovemaking prospered after my first use of Viagra. My erections are stronger, and they certainly last longer. My wife now attains climax regularly. We have intercourse almost every night and sometimes begin the following morning with more of the same.

We are jubilant lovers, each in our seventieth year. For my wife, there is a joy in sexual love that she had not known previously. For myself, confidence is fully restored.

This rave review comes from a usually unassuming man who rarely talks about his personal life—kind of like Bob Dole, who wanted to be president but who was too modest to talk about his days as a war hero. Now we see Dole's grinning visage almost daily on our television sets, extolling the benefits of a pharmaceutical uplift that restored his prowess in the bedroom.

Simply put, what has excited Bob Dole, Harry, and millions more just like them is a drug that enhances the body's natural system for creating erections, allowing the smooth muscles in the penis to relax and, in turn, allowing the organ to fill with blood.

HOW VIAGRA WORKS

Put more precisely, Viagra works on the chemical components of an erection, paving the way to eventual success. As we discussed earlier (see "How the Penis Works," Part III), there is a chain of chemical

interactions that is vital to achieving an erect penis. In the formula that
follows, we have inserted the role of Viagra.

> When a man is sexually stimulated, the chemical nitric oxide is
> released into two columns of erectile tissue in the penis called cor-
> pora cavernosa.
>
> Nitric oxide activates an enzyme, which then increases the levels of
> another chemical, cyclic guanosine monophosphate (cGMP).
>
> That chemical produces smooth-muscle relaxation in the corpora
> cavernosa and allows blood to flow into the penis.
>
> There is yet another chemical, called phosphodiesterase 5, or
> PDE5, that occurs naturally in and around nerve endings. It breaks
> down the cGMP in the corpora cavernosa.
>
> Viagra *inhibits* the PDE5. And when the PDE5 is inhibited, the
> cGMP, prompted by the nitric oxide and the enzyme, is enhanced,
> and more blood flows into the corpora cavernosa, sustaining an
> erection.

Before becoming available on the market as a prescription drug,
according to Pfizer Inc., Viagra was tested in more than four thousand
men. In twenty-one clinical trials, which included men with erectile
dysfunction that was diagnosed as mild, moderate, or complete, the
median age of patients was fifty-five. They had a broad range of conditions associated with ED, including high blood pressure, high cholesterol levels, diabetes, and prostate surgery. Patients had experienced
ED for an average of five years prior to entering the clinical trials.

Viagra was shown to be effective in approximately seven out of ten
men overall and was effective for patients with ED attributed to diabetes, spinal cord injury, or psychological causes, among others. Trial
results for patients and partners were assessed using questionnaires
designed with leading academic researchers, according to Pfizer.

You Need to Know

Patients taking nitrates in any form, including the heart medicine nitroglycerin, should not take Viagra.

Unlike other methods for treating impotence, Viagra won't "give" a man an erection. It *enables* him to have one. He must be stimulated.

It can take as long as an hour to become effective, but some men see results in twenty minutes.

More than 80 percent of prescriptions to date have been for men over the age of fifty.

Side effects occur in up to 10 percent of men. They include mild, temporary reactions such as flushed skin, headaches, upset stomach, and blue-tinted vision.

THE SAFETY FACTOR

Generally speaking, I believe that as long as a man *and his doctor* are aware of potential side effects, there should be no serious problems in taking Viagra. But it is important to keep in mind that the drug does not address every cause of impotence. And remember, impotence can be a symptom of some very serious health conditions or diseases like diabetes or heart disease. So it's necessary to have regular checkups. In fact, if a man hasn't had sex in awhile, and then he suddenly resumes, he could be setting himself up for a heart attack.

As for deaths caused by Viagra, let's put some exaggerated fears to rest by looking at a summary of reports provided by the Food and Drug Administration. From March through mid-November 1998, during which more than 50 million tablets were dispensed, the FDA received reports of 130 U.S. patients who died after having been prescribed Viagra.

Of the 130, two men died from homicide and drowning, three had strokes, and seventy-seven had cardiovascular events. Cause of death was unmentioned or unknown for forty-eight. Sixteen of the men took nitroglycerin or a nitrate medication that is not recommended with the use of Viagra. In addition, three were found with nitroglycerin in their possession, but it is not known if it was taken.

Excluding the two men who died from homicide and drowning, forty-four (34 percent) of the 128 patients died or had the onset of symptoms leading to death within four to five hours of Viagra use (including twenty-seven during or immediately after sexual intercourse). Six died or developed symptoms later the same day; eight, the next day; five, two days later; and four, three to seven days after Viagra use. The time from drug ingestion to death or onset of symptoms leading to death was not stated or was unknown for sixty-one men (48 percent).

Ninety (70 percent) of the 128 patients had one or more risk factors reported for cardiovascular or cerebrovascular disease (hypertension, hypercholesterolemia, cigarette smoking, diabetes mellitus, obesity, previous cardiac history).

Three additional persons without identified heart disease or risk factors had severe coronary artery disease detected at autopsy. Twelve were reported to have no previous history of cardiac disease or risk factors, but for ten of these, the time from last Viagra use to death or onset of symptoms leading to death was unknown or was at least two days later. Two men, sixty and seventy years old, had no mentioned risk factors, no sexual activity, and died shortly after Viagra ingestion.[37] Both the FDA and Pfizer say the death toll is low considering the large number of men who have taken it.

Those numbers make a pretty convincing case for the safety of the pill. But how about women?

VIAGRA FOR WOMEN

Women should have equal access to Viagra, and I think it will have the same beneficial effects on them that it does on men. Increased blood flow is just as important to the vagina or clitoris as it is to the penis in achieving sexual satisfaction. Many doctors already are prescribing the drug for women, although the FDA has not given its official sanction.

With millions of women suffering from some sort of sexual dysfunction, Viagra looks like an obvious answer to me. After all, women get blockage in arteries just like men do. Women smoke almost as much as men do. Women abuse alcohol, suffer from diabetes, use the same drugs, and ride on hard bicycle seats, too. They obviously deserve help as much as men.

Dr. Irwin Goldstein was one of the first doctors in the country to prescribe the drug for women. He talked on *Dateline NBC*[38] about a patient, one of the first women known to have Viagra prescribed for her. Her sex life had taken a dramatic turn for the worse after a partial hysterectomy. She said nothing was functioning normally, that her sex life was different, and that her body was different.

Then she took Viagra and was astonished at the results. "I couldn't believe the difference I felt. I was very surprised that it affected me that way. It really was remarkable."

Dr. Goldstein wasn't surprised, pointing out that Viagra works in men by affecting an enzyme that increases blood flow to the genitals and that the same enzyme is present in women. "If a woman has as her primary sexual problem diminished vaginal lubrication, pain, discomfort during sexual activity because of poor lubrication, and increased time to arouse, it seems logical to be able to try this in women," said Dr. Goldstein. He added that postmenopausal women who are aging, hypertensive, diabetic, and suffering from high cholesterol should be perfect candidates for Viagra.

I agree with Dr. Goldstein, but I also would like to point out another important benefit women can derive from Viagra. One of the best things about it is that a woman's participation is crucial to an enjoyable sexual encounter since the man must be stimulated in order for Viagra to work on him. The intimate prelude to intercourse always has been more important to women, and the success of the drug depends on satisfactory foreplay. I'd say that's a win-win situation.

One of my patients—let's call her Emily—lauds the benefits of Viagra without even taking it. In fact, I think she appreciates the results more than her husband. So let me tell you about this sixty-eight-year-old woman who experienced the onset of menopause eighteen years ago but who received no hormonal replacement therapy because she dreaded the possibility of breast cancer.

About three years ago, she finally started hormone replacement in small doses and gradually became more interested in sexual relations with her husband. Unfortunately, her husband suffered from impotence and couldn't satisfy her renewed urges. But they didn't give up. Within the past few months an examination revealed that his testosterone level was quite low, and he now is using testosterone patches, which have worked perfectly. But he still couldn't perform adequately until—*voila!*—he started taking Viagra.

The testosterone medication enhanced his desire, and Viagra helped produce the necessary erections. Today I can't get over the change I see in Emily. She looks better, feels better, and certainly is much happier as a result of this restored intimacy. I think there are a lot of women like Emily out there.

Meanwhile, research continues on the effects of Viagra on women. Dr. Jennifer Berman, a Boston-based urologist, recently conducted a study of seventeen postmenopausal women, some of whom were given Viagra and some a placebo. The drug appeared to increase physical arousal, but Berman cautioned that the sample size is small and that the study is ongoing.

Pfizer is conducting trials in Europe looking at the drug's effectiveness in both pre- and post-menopausal women. But the company doesn't recommend the medication for women until more data on safety and effectiveness is available. And let me add that women should not be tempted if Viagra is offered to them by friends or husbands. This is not a recreational drug. Please be cautious and talk to your doctor.

You Need to Know

1 Viagra is one of the least insured drugs available, with only about 40 percent of the prescriptions covered. I believe insurers, struggling with rising medical costs, worry more about the cost of the drug than safety.

2 The Veterans Administration won't make the drug available because it contends the pill is too expensive.

3 The Federal Aviation Administration recommends that pilots not take Viagra within six hours of flying because it could make it tough to distinguish between blues and greens found in cockpit instrument and runway lights.

4 Japan approved the sale of Viagra in record time, infuriating Japanese women who had been pushing for years to have birth control pill sales authorized. Approval of that pill finally came in June 1999, but women still are angry over the delay.

5 Men with erectile dysfunction caused by spinal-cord injuries are believed to be a group that will benefit greatly from taking Viagra. There are reports that 70 to 80 percent of men with SCI see improvement after taking the drug.

6 Some urologists say the growing recreational use by young, potent men should be discouraged because it could cause priapism, a persistent, painful erection that does not subside for several hours.

7 Because of some complaints about vision abnormalities, the University of Cologne in Germany tested five healthy volunteers with 100 mg. tablets of sildenafil. Tests of retinal function showed no effect on vision.

OTHER POSSIBILITIES

The only other oral drug currently available that is FDA-approved is yohimbine. The version of yohimbine that's available by prescription is a chemical relative of one of the few folk remedies that has proved effective to any useful degree. For centuries, people in Africa and India have used yohimbine, which is made from tree bark, as an aphrodisiac.

As a treatment for impotence, yohimbine works two ways: First, it helps prevent the sympathetic nervous system from inhibiting the man's erection. Second, it helps to increase the flow of blood to the penis.

Not everyone agrees on just how effective yohimbine is in treating impotence, and it does have some serious side effects, like a sudden increase in blood pressure. I strongly recommend that if a man is interested in trying it, he should see his doctor for a prescription—and to discuss possible interactions and side effects. Some men might think they can get around this by going to the health food store and buying herbal preparations or even topical lotions, but they are a waste of money.

Aphrodite, the Goddess of Love

Which brings us to aphrodisiacs—food, drink, drug, scent, or a device that supposedly enhances sexual desire. Outlandish claims have been made for anchovies, licorice, scallops, Spanish fly, and myriad other exotic items. Let me be emphatic—the reputed sexual boost from so-called aphrodisiacs is not based on fact. It's pure folklore.

The Food and Drug Administration declared in 1989 that there is no scientific proof that any over-the-counter aphrodisiacs work to treat sexual dysfunction. Rhinoceros horn and oysters have been touted as performance enhancers, as was chocolate before its use became common. There is no evidence that any of them work.

A good example is the rhinoceros horn, which, because of its similarity in shape to the penis, has a worldwide reputation as a libido booster. Here are the facts. The horn contains significant amounts of calcium and phosphorus which, when added to a poor diet, possibly could improve physical vigor. American diets are not lacking in those ingredients, and adding ground rhino horn would have no effect on anyone in a modern society.

Please read Part V for an appreciation of the most powerful aphrodisiacs of all—a clear mind and a healthy lifestyle.

WHAT ABOUT THE FUTURE?

There are other oral medications with possibilities in treating impotence, but the most promising ones aren't available yet in the United States. One of these is called phentolamine, which is an oral version of a drug that has been used in injection form. This works by dilating the arteries and relaxing the smooth-muscle tissue, but it may cause a drop in blood pressure and a condition called tachycardia, which means a rapid heartbeat. The FDA is still reviewing phentolamine.

Another drug that's being studied is spontane, an oral apomorphine. This is best suited for men whose impotence is largely psychological since it works by helping the brain process the stimuli that would cause an erection.

Then there is phentolamine, which is manufactured by Zonagen Inc. of Houston under the trade name of Vasomax. Although not approved yet in this country, it is available by prescription in Mexico under the name Z-max. Zonagen is hoping for FDA approval by the end of 1999.

Testing of Vasomax indicates that it acts faster in producing erections than Viagra, but that about 10 percent of the men tested suffered headaches, facial flushing, and nasal congestion. Researchers from Boston University School of Medicine reported that 34 percent of those taking 40 mg. of Vasomax and 45 percent taking 80 mg. showed improvement in their ability to have an erection. They also noted that

Vasomax appears to have less of an impact on desire than Viagra, but that the physical effect of the erection is the same.

In tests conducted by TAP Holdings Inc., of Deerfield, Illinois, men taking apomorphine also showed significant improvement in their ability to achieve an erection sufficient for intercourse. The side effects included nausea in up to 39 percent of those taking a high dosage of the experimental drug.[39]

Pfizer, which has a huge $2 billion research budget, is working on a second pill that would be as capable as Viagra but without the potential side effects. Pfizer also is working on a version of Viagra that could be slipped under the tongue in wafer form and dissolve within seconds. If the faster-acting form is successful, it would allow patients to take Viagra only minutes before sex. Pfizer officials say that any new version of Viagra is still years away.

Time-Tested Treatments

- MUSE
- INJECTION THERAPY
- IMPLANTS
- VACUUM PUMPS
- TESTOSTERONE TREATMENT
- VASCULAR SURGERY

There's a man named George who was left largely impotent by a prostate operation about five years ago. He and his wife, both of them in their sixties, had enjoyed an active sex life and obviously didn't want to give it up, so George's urologist prescribed penile injections. They worked but not to the couple's satisfaction.

"I'd trudge back to the kitchen before going to bed, raid the refrigerator, fill up a syringe, and then inject myself. Meanwhile, my wife's enjoying a good book before going to sleep and wondering what the hell I'm doing banging around in the kitchen. Then she had to make a choice between what I had to offer and the good book. It wasn't easy for either of us."

You can bet that George jumped on the Viagra bandwagon with gusto when the drug finally was approved. Despite the low incidence of side effects, he unfortunately is one of the unlucky ones. "My heart beat faster, my face was burning up, and I felt so damn jumpy I couldn't stand it," was his reaction to taking Viagra. Poor George! It's back to late-night trips to the refrigerator.

And George has a lot of company. Once sildenafil hit the market there was a widespread expectation that existing treatments would be eliminated. No more injections, pumps, patches, suppositories, and implants. But that hasn't been the case. Viagra, although wildly successful, does not work for many thousands of men, who fortunately have other options.

MUSE

In 1996, the FDA approved a suppository that a man could insert into his penis to produce an erection. Muse, which stands for "medicated urethral system for erection," was welcomed by many men as a much more convenient, comfortable way to treat their impotence. The pellet contains alprostadil and is delivered by an applicator about an inch deep into the urethra at the tip of the penis, resulting in an erection usually within ten minutes and lasting up to sixty minutes.

Clinical trials show Muse to be effective for about 65 percent of those who use it. The erections that are achieved by using Muse are sometimes less than desired, but usually they are at least sufficient for intercourse. Doctors who prescribe Muse say results are much more impressive with those patients who have been well educated in the use of the product and whose spouses are included in the process.

Men who have used Muse successfully after trying injections, clearly prefer inserting the pellet to plunging a needle into their penises. But there is somewhat of a downside to using Muse. The penis must be massaged for about ten seconds while the pellet dissolves, and using the applicator has been a problem for some men. Also, lying down is not recommended, especially on the back, during the first few minutes after the pellet has been inserted because that would reduce blood flow to the penis. Men are advised to stand or walk during this period, which is hardly conducive to lovemaking.

Side effects include aching in the penis, testicles, and the area between the penis and rectum. Some men also have reported a burning sensation in the urethra, redness of the penis due to increased blood flow, and minor urethral bleeding or spotting. Low blood pressure also is a risk. Although erections sometimes last longer than necessary, the suppositories are less risky than injections, for example, and they can be used more frequently.

Vivus Inc., which makes Muse, has been on a financial rollercoaster thanks to the advent of Viagra. In 1997, Muse was the top-selling product for impotence, with 475,000 patients using it. In fact, the company was barely able to keep up with increasing demand. Product revenue reached $33.5 million in the second quarter of 1997, but for the second quarter of 1998 it had dropped to $16 million. Prescriptions fell from fifteen thousand a week to five thousand a week. The stock price plunged from $37 a share to the $7 range during the same period—all thanks to the booming launch of Viagra.

That's a dramatic example of the impact Viagra has had on the industry. Given a choice, swallowing a pill obviously is much more pleasant than inserting a suppository in the penis. But Muse remains an excellent alternative if Viagra doesn't do the trick. Vivus management believes it has a future with those for whom Viagra doesn't work, including men with heart conditions, diabetes, postsurgical trauma, pelvis injury, and complete inability to achieve an erection.

INJECTION THERAPY

Another option is self-injection therapy, which is exactly what it sounds like. The man injects his penis with a medication causing it to become engorged with blood and erect. Injection therapy, which has been around for some time, is as close as you can get to a sure-fire solution to impotence. But it can produce some painful side effects.

Papaverine, a powerful vasodilator and muscle relaxant, was the first drug to be used for injections. The next drug to come on the market was alprostadil, a synthetic version of a naturally occurring hormone, prostaglandin E1. In 1995, the FDA approved Caverject, which made alprostadil available by prescription in premixed units. Then in 1997, a slightly different version was approved under the brand name Edex.

Alprostadil works by relaxing the smooth-muscle tissue so that blood can flow into the penis. The man receives his first injection at the doctor's office, and then after learning the technique, he is able to inject himself. It's an effective treatment, producing an erection in about 94 percent of the men who use it.

One study reported 65 percent improvement in men more than seventy years old who had not achieved an erection in three years. It also is effective in men with a wide range of medical disorders, including diabetes, surgery, and injury. Alprostadil has a lower risk for side effects than other drugs used for this treatment, but half of the men in one study experienced some burning and pain at the injection site.

The erections produced are very firm and long lasting, but there are some drawbacks. For one thing, they are painful. Also, they should be used only about twice a week. In addition, fibrous tissue can build up at the injection site, and the penis can become deformed.

Some men develop priapism, a condition in which the erection does not subside and which in some cases requires medical attention. In one major study only 1 percent of men experienced erections lasting more than four hours, and all but two cases were resolved without treatment.

Men whose impotence is caused by leakage in the blood vessels, and those who are taking medications that thin the blood, should not use injection therapy. And, despite its general success, self-injection therapy has a high dropout rate. In one study of men either taking papaverine or prostaglandin E1, only 20 percent were still using the treatment after an average of eleven months. More than half stopped using it because they lost interest in the procedure. Some decided to try other treatments, while others dropped out because of side effects or because their partners objected.

Despite all this, injection therapy has been a boon for many patients. Not everyone experiences the side effects, and many couples have learned to make a game of the procedure. The results often can be very impressive.

Finally, both the injections and the Muse method are best for someone who's really motivated and not too squeamish. But they are even more expensive than Viagra. They each cost about $25 per dose, which amounts to about $2,600 a year if used twice a week. That's more than double the cost of Viagra, which would run $1,040 a year if someone used two pills a week.

IMPLANTS

For some men, penile implants have been the answer. One of the first implants to be developed has been around for more than twenty years. It's a semi-rigid device that consists of a pair of bendable silicone rods. The penis is permanently erect as a result—the man has to keep it folded down his thigh most of the time, and when he wants an erection for sex, he simply pulls it up into position. Aside from the obvious disadvantage of a perpetual erection, this method does not increase the overall size of the penis the way a normal erection would.

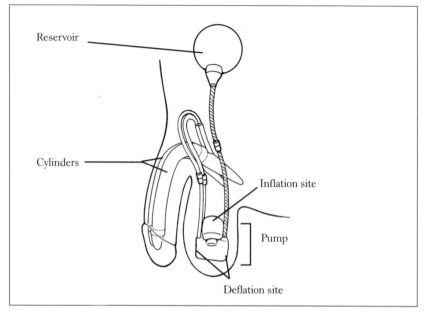

Reservoir

Cylinders

Inflation site

Pump

Deflation site

Inflatable penile prosthesis inside your body

Fortunately, there are newer types of implants available that involve an inflatable device that is pumped with fluid in order to make the penis erect. The basic version inflates when the end of the implant rod is squeezed and is later deflated by manipulating the base of the rod. Unfortunately, this type of implant can deflate during intercourse as well.

A newer version is a two-piece system that involves a pump and a reservoir being implanted in the base of the scrotum. Two cords or cylinders go into the penis, through the corpora cavernosa, and liquid from the reservoir is pumped into them. The man squeezes the scrotum to open the valve and to pump the liquid. Then later, he squeezes the scrotum again in a different place to deflate the erection.

The latest version involves a three-piece system in which a liquid reservoir is implanted in the abdomen. The reservoir is connected by a tube to the inflate/deflate valve, which is implanted into the base of the scrotum. As in the earlier version, two cylinders are implanted in the shaft of the penis. This prosthesis achieves the most natural erection of the three, increasing the length and the diameter of the penis more effectively than the others. Also, it maintains sensation better than the other versions because it's less likely to disrupt the interaction between the prostate and the testicles.

The device is filled with normal saline, which is compatible with body fluid. Also, the cylinders are designed to allow lengthening, the extent of which is limited by how much the tissue will handle. And the inflate/deflate pump and cylinder components are packaged already connected to each other so that during surgery, the urologist only needs to connect the tubing between the reservoir and the cylinders.

Anyone considering even the most sophisticated of these prostheses should know that the erection produced probably will be different than his original, natural erections. Included could be a shorter penis, less firmness, less width, and possibly reduced sensation. Also, the glans (the tip of the penis) may be soft because the device will not provide rigidity in that area. It also should be understood that implanting a prosthesis likely will damage or destroy any remaining natural ability to have an erection. That means that if the prosthesis is removed, there probably won't be any possibility of having any kind of a natural erection.

Following surgery, it usually is recommended that four to six weeks be allowed for complete healing and before attempting intercourse. Resuming sex too soon can result in pain or infection, but if everything goes smoothly, and the urologist's recommendations are followed, the benefit is the ability to have an erection as often as desired. An added bonus should be the involvement of a partner in the inflation process, incorporating that into the lovemaking routine. After all, this is all about restoring sexual intimacy.

It's difficult to state categorically that these implants are always worth the trouble and expense that accompany them. Each man, and each couple, is different. It's true that penile implants are the most expensive option of all. Generally, they run ten thousand to fifteen thousand dollars for everything, and they're not always covered by insurance. But there's no question that implants are effective. About 90 percent of the surgeries are successful, and men who undergo these procedures report relatively few problems. The operations generally require only a local anesthetic and often are done on an outpatient basis.

Occasionally, the implants have to be removed if there's an infection or adverse reaction, or they might have to be replaced if they start to leak fluid. But those are just minor risks that should not stand in the way if a couple decides that an implant is the best option, and if a man's doctor thinks he's a good candidate for the surgery.

For some men, and some couples, intercourse is a high priority. I think that for them, the implants can produce psychological satisfaction that other methods might not offer. They also might boost the man's self-esteem and help restore a degree of intimacy in the relationship.

Every year about twenty thousand men undergo penile implants. For those who are diabetic or who have nerve damage from other causes, such as prostate surgery, it may be the best option. And for men who have severe vascular destruction, an implant may be the only way to produce an erection. But surgery is still surgery, and it has a risk factor. That's why I feel strongly that most men would be better off if they tried the less-invasive methods first, saving surgery as a last resort.

A Success Story

Most women who confide in me blame themselves for the loss of intimacy with their husbands. It's a natural tendency to look at ourselves before we realize that the true scope of a problem might be beyond us. But this inner focus of guilt can have serious consequences.

Gladys, who had been my patient for many years, was a classic example. She developed breast cancer at forty-eight, ended up with a radical mastectomy, and was dealing with menopause at the same time. The combination was terribly depressing for her, especially the disfiguring surgery. Complicating her problem was her husband's reaction. Any physical affection between them had slowly vanished.

Having met John, and thanks to my increasing awareness of the widespread impact of impotence among my patients, I invited him to join us at his wife's next appointment. Together, we quickly became acutely aware of the actual dimensions of their problem. John was suffering from hypertension, and his lifestyle had all the ingredients for a disastrous love life—too much food, booze, and little physical activity. As I had suspected, his wife's situation had almost nothing to do with his loss of sexual appetite.

With the assistance of his personal physician, John changed his eating habits and began a good exercise program, which did wonders for his health. But the restoration of what once had been an active sex life with Gladys came with the help of a fine urologist friend of mine. Those were the days before Viagra, but a penile implant solved John's problem and certainly helped save his marriage. And years later, the implanted device has become such a natural part of their lovemaking that they won't consider any alternatives.

VACUUM PUMPS

The least invasive of all the methods currently available for treating impotence are vacuum devices. External management systems, as they are properly called, are 95 percent effective, safe, and simple to use for all forms of impotence—except when severe scarring has occurred as with Peyronie's disease (see page 95, Part III).

Simply put, the penis is placed inside a plastic cylinder, a vacuum is created, and blood is caused to flow into the penis. The erections are very natural in appearance as well as feel, and the pumps can be used several times a day. None of the pumps on the market costs even a fraction of what a penile implant would cost. In fact, at about $500, they're cheaper than any method available—injections, Muse, or Viagra—and they don't have any of the side effects associated with some other treatments.

Now, let's examine exactly how external vacuum therapy works. A pump is used along with a hollow cylinder into which the penis is placed. Activation of the vacuum pump draws blood into the penis, which causes an erection. The erection is maintained by a rubber ring—a constriction band—placed at the base of the penis, which prevents blood from draining. When the ring is removed, the penis returns to its soft state.

There's a device on the market that uses a battery-powered pump to draw the blood into the penis instead of a manual pump. This version is a single unit, so it's a more streamlined design. This is the ErecAid System™ incorporating the Osbon Technique of vacuum therapy.[40] It features a lifetime warranty against defects or breakage on the pump and cylinder. Medicare and most private insurers cover the cost. Other devices include Catalyst and the VED pump.

As I said, the vacuum pumps give a man a natural-feeling erection as well as the best possible control. Still, some men, perhaps 25 percent, stop using their pumps after just a few months. They complain that it's not spontaneous enough, and others find the rubber ring to be painful. Also, some men, particularly if they're not in a stable, long-term relationship, might find the pump to be a little awkward. However, many men and women have overcome their inhibitions regarding the pump and have gone on to develop rewarding sexual relationships.

I understand the need for spontaneity, but it only takes three to five minutes to produce an erection in most cases. Many couples, after initial apprehension, have found the

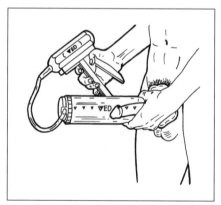

Vacuum pump to create an erection

results to be highly satisfactory. In a study of men who had used the vacuum device for many years, almost 79 percent reported improvement in their relationships with their sexual partners, and 83 percent said they had intercourse whenever they chose.

A word of caution—it is very important to use a medically approved pump because there have been reports of injury from vacuum devices bought through catalogs that do not have a pressure-release valve or other safety elements. See your doctor for guidance.

TESTOSTERONE TREATMENT

Testosterone, the male sex hormone, has been blamed for everything from rape to road rage to low intelligence, but it's going through an impressive rehabilitation these days. In fact, it increasingly is being prescribed for men and women with low libidos without fear that it will adversely affect their mood or temperament.

So what is this hormone that so often has been a scapegoat for various ills in our society? It's produced in the testicles and ovaries and, to a lesser degree, in the adrenal glands. It is responsible for determining the biological differences between the sexes—men have eight to ten times more than women do, and levels drop naturally as both sexes age. The amount in the blood varies from person to person and from hour to hour. It is higher in the morning and lower at night. Extreme surpluses or deficiencies are rare.[41]

The latest thinking is that this vital hormone affects behavior and is the juice that fuels libido, but there is no proof that it causes aggression. However, certain behavior can produce a testosterone surge. In separate studies of chess players and soccer fans, testosterone levels shot up in the victors and plunged in the losers after the matches. So we're obviously talking about a powerful force in the human body.

Testosterone therapy is usually limited to men with hypogonadism (testosterone deficiency) and is not recommended for men with testosterone levels that are normal for their age. Some experts believe it may be helpful for older men whose levels are deficient and that it might improve sexual drive. (There are indications that testosterone levels decline from 30 to 40 percent in men from their late forties to their early seventies.)

Men with known or suspected prostate cancer should not use testosterone treatment. While it hasn't been shown to cause prostate cancer, testosterone replacement therapy may promote the growth of existing prostate cancer. As a result, prostate cancer should be ruled out in older patients or others at high risk before attempting testosterone replacement therapy.

Oral forms are not recommended because of the risk of liver damage when taken over long periods of time. Injections are used in some cases, but testosterone now can be administered through skin patches. The first patch, Testoderm, must be applied to the skin of the scrotum every twenty-four hours. A newer patch, Androderm, however, may be applied to either the abdomen, back, thighs, or upper arm. In one study, the patches restored normal testosterone levels in about 90 percent of the subjects.

The Androderm transdermal system delivers its medication through the skin in a five-milligram oval patch with a testosterone gel-filled reservoir in the middle. One patch continues delivering testosterone for about twenty-four hours in a pattern that closely mimics the natural way testosterone rises and falls. Unlike the scrotal patch, Androderm can be worn during sex and while showering or exercising. But it can cause skin irritation or allergic skin reactions.

It is estimated that most of the more than 5 million American men believed to be testosterone deficient remain untreated, placing them at risk for long-term medical consequences. Symptoms of a deficiency include sexual dysfunction (loss of libido and impotence) fatigue, depressed mood, muscle wasting, osteoporosis (loss of bone tissue), and the absence of or regression of sexual characteristics such as muscle development, deep voice, and male hair distribution.

But it's very important to remember that a depressed level of testosterone is the culprit in very few cases of true impotence—actually only about 5 percent. Clinical impotence is not the same thing as a drop in libido. The word "impotence" really describes a condition in which a man cannot achieve or sustain an erection. He very well may have the desire, but he just can't do it. Most of the time, impotence is caused by vascular or nerve problems that have nothing to do with testosterone. And conversely, there are some men with abnormally low testosterone levels who can perform just fine.

If a man really thinks the problem is his libido, he should visit with his doctor, get a diagnosis, and ask about the patches we've described. This is a mostly safe and effective treatment for men who truly have low levels of testosterone. For most men, however, supplemental testosterone just isn't the answer. In fact, for healthy men, it isn't recommended at all.

VASCULAR SURGERY

For men whose impotence is caused by damage to the arteries or blood vessels, vascular surgery might be an option. Two types of operations are available: revascularization (or bypass) surgery and venous igation. The American Urologic Association stresses that vascular surgery is still investigative.

The revascularization procedure is effected by taking an artery from a leg and then surgically connecting it to the arteries at the back of the penis, bypassing the blockages and restoring blood flow. Young men with local sites of arterial blockage generally achieve the best results. In studies of selected patients there was improvement in 50 percent to 75 percent after five years.

Venous ligation is performed when the penis is unable to store a sufficient amount of blood to maintain an erection. This operation ties off or removes veins that are causing an excessive amount of blood to drain from the erection chambers. Success rate is estimated between 40 percent and 50 percent initially, but drops to 15 percent over the long term.

Choosing a Treatment

Often, a man—or his wife—might be hesitant to try something like a vacuum pump or even an implant because they remember better times and fear that things won't be the same sexually. One of the most common concerns is that the man won't have the same sensations he had before he became impotent. The truth is that often the man can achieve an orgasm using these methods—as long as the brain can still transmit the message of stimulation and as long as the ejaculatory fluid can follow its path.

Having said that, I think we should keep in mind that what's normal for one man might not be normal for another. There are men who actually have orgasms without ejaculating, and there are men who have orgasms with an ejaculation but who never do achieve a full erection. So even if a man's erection is produced or enhanced by one of these devices, even if it's not like it used to be, that doesn't mean he can't achieve sexual satisfaction.

I know there are cases where the erection is purely a mechanical achievement because the vascular or neurological damage is so severe. But even in these situations, if a man wants to satisfy his wife, it can help his self-esteem and his relationship if he can have intercourse with her.

Even if a man cannot achieve an erection or an orgasm, there are many ways that a couple can give to each other. They can still have a great degree of intimacy without pharmaceutical or mechanical assistance. Regaining intimacy is what most couples are concerned about, and rightfully so. For some couples this means regaining the ability to have intercourse, but that is not a priority for everyone.

Choosing the right treatment for impotence is a decision that a man and his wife must make in conjunction with a doctor and after careful consideration of their own priorities. Medical decisions always should be made in the context of a much broader definition of sexuality, which includes emotional and psychological factors as well.

Taking the Initiative

- How to Bring Up the Subject
- When the Cause is Psychological
- Home Experiments
- What to Expect at the Doctor's Office
- If Further Testing is Prescribed

By now you've learned a lot about health and impotence, especially as it pertains to men. By examining my findings, you've already taken a significant step toward a solution to the problem, and I congratulate you for the progress you've made. We know that overcoming fear and ignorance can lead to solutions for long-suffering people, and doing so merely requires your being inquisitive and aggressive.

The first step I recommend for any woman confronting the impotence of her husband or partner is to confirm for him the fact that there is hope. In fact, it is fair to say that the vast majority of cases can be treated successfully by using the various methods we have available today. This must be made abundantly clear to anyone suffering impotence. And I recommend using this book as a tool in making the point.

Next, a woman and her husband should discuss the situation openly and together make an honest assessment of his symptoms. The goal of this analysis is to clear the way for an appointment with a doctor. Remember, most men are quite reluctant to see a doctor about anything, and if the problem is impotence, they are doubly unlikely to seek help. The secret is a caring woman who is willing to lead the way.

HOW TO BRING UP THE SUBJECT

It's extremely hard for a woman to bring up a difficult subject like this, especially if the husband has refused to talk about it over a long period of time—which is typical. Often when a couple has been coping with impotence for years, a lot of anger, frustration, and pain can build up. Connie Engels, the sex therapist we have referred to many times, counsels women who need to bring up problems with their husbands, and she has some important recommendations.

First, she suggests that women find a way to keep their own feelings on the back burner. Remember that the aim is to encourage the husband to talk, not to explain the wife's personal difficulties. Also, Ms. Engels suggests that the woman concentrate on listening to whatever he has to say without minimizing his feelings in any way. Only after he's finished talking should the wife attempt to restate what he said just to confirm that he was fully understood.

This may take time and several attempts at discussion, Ms. Engels says. In fact, she believes a wife always should listen carefully to her husband's feelings over the course of several conversations before restating them. Then she can go on to suggest some options. The time also might be ripe to mention a few things that can be tried, such as visiting with his doctor to rule out any illnesses, or scheduling an appointment with a sex therapist, or even reading a good book on the subject.

The point is that the husband should be encouraged to make some choices, to begin to take control of his problem. If none of this works over a long period of time, then I strongly suggest that the wife—on her own—consult with a sex therapist to get some support and new ideas. Keep in mind that the goal is to encourage the husband to see his doctor so that both partners can have some peace of mind regarding his health—and so that any physical cause of impotence can be determined.

Let's say all of these steps have been taken, that the cause of impotence has been revealed, and that a successful treatment has been achieved. I believe both of you still might find it helpful to see a sex therapist or a psychotherapist. Your relationship has come through a bumpy period that can strain any relationship. And renewal of sexual activity usually requires adjustments that can delay the full restoration of passion and excitement in a marriage. Professional help probably is the answer.

WHEN THE CAUSE IS PSYCHOLOGICAL

It's not easy to enter therapy either alone or with your spouse. But for a couple to regain a satisfying sex life, it might be necessary—and it should be rewarding! Therapy can alleviate problems that naturally occur when sexual activity is resumed. But it's also important to know that male impotence can be caused by a psychological problem, not just the physical difficulties we have discussed in detail.

It is necessary to consider such contributing factors as clinical depression, a childhood history of sexual abuse, or sexual compulsions. It also is very important for a man to feel that he is satisfying his wife. If there is even a hint that he is not, it can have dire consequences. For a man, the biggest relationship threat is what I would call emasculation. If a marriage has deteriorated to the point where the man is made to feel inferior, especially with respect to his sexual performance, then he actually could become impotent. In a case like this, the intimacy, the love, and the acceptance between the partners has deteriorated so badly that both of them may need counseling.

In order to benefit from therapy, a couple needs to be very honest with each other. If a man is cheating on his wife, for example, he may feel too guilty to perform. Sometimes a man might lose interest in his wife after they've been married awhile or after their children are born because he doesn't see wives and mothers as sexual beings.

Problems like these need to be worked out with a therapist because they not only can destroy a relationship, they also can lead to impotence. Of course, the man must have the desire to seek help for himself in order for the therapy to have any benefit. And the couple must be willing to face the issue together with total honesty, love, and respect.

HOME EXPERIMENTS

There are a few things that a man can do on his own just to get a sense of whether there's a physical reason for his impotence—and what that might be. But it's important not to let this drag on too long without medical attention since impotence can be a symptom of so many other conditions.

One thing a man can do is determine whether he can achieve a full erection by himself, without his partner. People try to measure these things in all sorts of ways, but any man knows what a full erection means for him. If the man can get a full erection by himself, then he knows his body is functioning properly.

Remember how we talked about the mechanics of an erection? If he can produce an erection on his own, we know that the man's brain is transmitting the message of stimulation, and that the message is being received. We then know that the smooth-muscle tissue in the penis is able to relax and let the blood flow in. We also know that his vascular system is functioning well enough to keep the blood there.

And, finally, we know that there is no "leakage" of the blood back into the body until the man has an orgasm.

What all this means is that if the man who has passed this self-test is impotent when he's trying to make love with his wife, then there is some other reason—his body is working just fine. Maybe at this point he can start thinking about whether he has psychological problems, and perhaps he can ask his primary-care physician to refer him to a psychotherapist.

There are a few other "experiments" that a man and woman can perform together that could prove to be beneficial in more ways than one. You need to be able to discern if there's been any nerve damage. And, who knows, you might even have some fun participating in these experiments.

First, the woman can take an object like a pencil or a feather and rub it on her partner's upper inner thigh. At the same time, watch whether the testicle rises. If it does, then his reflexes are working properly. A couple of other tests can be tried, but that's the most pleasant one that comes to mind. Another way is to apply ice to the testicle and check whether it rises. Then there's another quick test that the husband might not want to try, but it's an excellent way to check out all the nearby nerves. The woman inserts a gloved finger into the man's rectum and at the same time pinches the end of his penis or taps it hard. If the rectum contracts around your finger, then the nerves are probably intact.

If you don't get those reactions—if the testicles don't move, or if the rectum does not contract—then your husband should see a doctor right away because there could be serious neurological damage.

There are a few ways to test for vascular damage, too. Of course, it's always a good idea to monitor your cardiovascular health, and many men and women already know whether they have problems with their heart or their circulation. But a good way to start is simply by taking a walk. And this is something a couple can do together. What you do is walk at least a mile at a fairly brisk pace. Even if a little winded, he should be able to carry on a conversation—otherwise slow down a little. The idea is to determine how well his body processes oxygen—a process called "oxygenation."

If he develops a sharp pain in either or both calves, it could indicate poor oxygenation, which may mean that the blood flow to the lower extremities is impaired. Of course, it doesn't necessarily indicate a problem with the blood flowing to the penis, but it is a good indication of the man's overall cardiovascular health.

In addition, there are some common-sense indicators that the flow of blood to the penis is impaired. One indicator would be whether the man's penis is constantly cold. Some men notice that their penis isn't as warm as it should be, even if they're using a heating pad or if they otherwise feel warm enough. This could indicate that the blood supply to the penis is inadequate. Also, a bluish color could indicate the same problem.

Another way for a man to examine himself is by touch. The penis should not have any hard, firm areas when it isn't erect. The man should check everywhere, including the sides and the base of the penis. If there is a hard spot, that could indicate a calcification or a fibrosis in the vascular cavities of the penis. This condition is caused by the gradual accumulation of plaque, the same way it can build up in the arteries that surround and supply the heart. If the blood flow to the heart is impeded, the person will develop coronary heart disease and eventually have a heart attack. If the patient develops artery disease elsewhere, it can result in a stroke, among other things. And if the blood flow to the penis is impeded, it can definitely result in impotence.

If the man suspects any calcification, he should schedule an appointment immediately with his doctor. This could be a sign of some very serious cardiovascular disease.

Assuming that the impotence is caused by a physical problem of some sort, then the best place to start is with the primary-care physician. For most men, that's usually an internist or a family doctor. In the process of conducting a complete physical, the doctor will be able to tell whether a urologist, an endocrinologist, or a cardiologist should be consulted.

The patient should be prepared to discuss any medications he might be taking, including over-the-counter products, vitamins, herbs, or other dietary supplements. This might take some thought, so I would encourage making up a list before the appointment. Even seemingly unimportant use of aspirin or a multivitamin should be included.

For example, maybe the man bought some kind of herbal product that's being touted as an aphrodisiac, and he quickly learned that it didn't work. He should include that on his list anyway because it could give the doctor some insight into his condition—and because it may have interacted with another drug he was taking at the time.

He also should include any illegal drugs he might have taken at any point in his life as well as his smoking and drinking habits. He should reveal any drug therapy or other substances he might have used specifically to improve his sexual performance—especially whether he's ever considered or actually used injections, pumps, or implants.

Finally, the man should be prepared to answer general questions and to give a family history. And if this seems like a lot of advance preparation, that's because it is extremely important. The more information the patient can provide, the more helpful the doctor can be.

WHAT TO EXPECT AT THE DOCTOR'S OFFICE

It's important for a man to have a complete physical on a regular basis and not wait for severe symptoms such as impotence to pop up before acting. And if he is having regular physicals, and he's having even minor problems with his erections or his libido, there is no excuse for not mentioning it to the doctor instead of waiting until he can't perform at all.

But even if it's gotten to the point of impotence, and this is the first checkup he's had in years, there's every reason to be optimistic because, as we've said many times, there are so many treatments available. He'll also need to have his hormone levels checked because testosterone deficiencies and elevated estrogen levels definitely can cause a drop in a man's libido. And hormone problems are very treatable.

During a complete physical, blood pressure will be measured, which will indicate whether hypertension is involved. He also probably will be given a stress test, which should give an indication of cardiovascular health. All of these conditions can affect a man's sexual health, and they're very serious in and of themselves.

IF FURTHER TESTING IS PRESCRIBED

If the primary-care physician decides that a visit with a urologist is in order, then the man can expect some additional tests to see whether his penis is working properly. For example, the urologist may decide to do an arteriography. This involves injecting dye into the arteries of the penis to check the flow of blood. It's very similar to the way that cardiologists examine the coronary arteries. Another common test involves injecting a substance called papaverine into the penis, which tells the doctor whether the blood vessels are capable of expanding. It's a way of gauging any arteriosclerosis or hardening of the arteries.

Certain symptoms can raise a red flag that diabetes may be a possibility. If you tell the doctor that you're urinating every half hour, and you just can't seem to quench your thirst—then it's probably safe to assume you're diabetic or close to it. Now, that's different than the person who has to get up once at night to urinate. That patient probably isn't diabetic, at least not yet.

When your family doctor takes your history, he or she will be watching for all of these different health conditions: diabetes, hypertension, heart disease, vascular disease, even problems that may not occur to you right away, like a tendency of the blood to clot too quickly.

The doctor will take both urine samples and blood samples in order to measure the level of glucose in your body. This would indicate whether the pancreas is functioning as it should and is producing enough insulin. An elevated glucose level can be caused by several different factors. But if it's severely elevated, you might be diagnosed with diabetes. If it's slightly elevated, again, depending on other factors, you'll probably be given a fasting blood sugar test. This would entail fasting all night, and then taking a urine and blood sample in the morning. Maybe it will turn out that you're not diabetic yet. Or maybe you'll have adult-onset diabetes that can be managed without drugs.

The point is that it's very important to be aware of symptoms and to report them to your doctor. Unfortunately, a lot of people don't pay attention until it's too late. Diabetes and other diseases are life threatening if they are not diagnosed, and they often can lead to impotence if not treated.

It is worth repeating that impotence not only is a demoralizing experience for both a man and his partner, it can signal other serious health problems. If there is an underlying illness, it can be diagnosed and treated. And even if there isn't an illness, solutions for almost any case of impotence are available for those who seek them. There is nothing to lose and everything to gain.

Part V

A Healthy Lifestyle

A Healthy Lifestyle

- THE SEX CONNECTION
- THE PROPER DIET
- CHOOSING SUPPLEMENTS
- THE IMPORTANCE OF EXERCISE

Americans are dazzled constantly by golden images of abundant good health. We worship those gorgeous bodies slinking across our television screens, wishing we were just like them. We revere the beautiful people who smile on us from the incessant world of advertising, envying their perfection. And we idolize our muscular sports heroes, reaping vicarious joy from their amazing feats. Even our daily routines are crammed with healthy reminders.

Walking down the aisle at the supermarket, I see on either side of me piles of low-fat this, fat-free that, healthy this, nutritious that. The produce section is even more impressive. Beautifully formed vegetables and fruits nestle in glistening stacks of wholesome perfection. The Garden of Eden must have looked like this! But there's more. On the way out I walk by the magazine rack and take in the glowing faces and the captivating curves. Clever titles trumpet the joys of living the good life by dieting and exercising our way to rapturous good health. Everybody is tan, happy, and strong. But is that the *real* world?

Now, come with me to the airport, and let's do some *real* people watching. Milling about, looking tense and tired, are squadrons of mostly overweight people, some dragging along their chubby children. They stare dazedly at monitors, sway like elephants while standing in line, or collapse in chairs that are too small for their bulges. Arrayed along the main corridor are neon invitations to buy some fries, try a cheeseburger, or how about a nice chocolate sundae? And bellying up to the counters are more nervous, overweight people bent on calming themselves with calories.

Then there's sex. Actually sex, sex, and more sex. Are we a nation of libidos run amok? Judging by what we see and read there is nothing else on our minds. We live in the information age, and much of what peppers our consciousness is a sexual message of some kind. Sex sells everything— cars, planes, boats, cereal, soup, and soap. There's no escaping it.

But there also is no ignoring the *truth* of it all. Most of us are overweight, drink too much, have poor diet habits, take too many drugs, and suffer sexual dysfunction at an alarming rate. We have the most money, the best of foods, the most sophisticated medical care, and the knowledge to make us the healthiest people on earth. But we're among the least healthy of the world's advanced nations, surpassing many of them in diseases and ailments that can be attributed directly to our lifestyles.

For example, we know that impotence is on a rampage among us, with millions of men and women affected. We also are learning that a majority of those cases could have been avoided or certainly altered by eating properly, controlling alcohol and drug consumption, eliminating smoking, and exercising enough to ensure a strong cardiovascular system. It sounds simple and it is. So let me help you appreciate how a healthy lifestyle can bolster your sense of well-being and improve your ability to enjoy an intimate relationship.

THE SEX CONNECTION

As you know, vascular problems are one of the most common causes of impotence. A diet high in fat, especially saturated fats and trans fats, can contribute to this problem by increasing the levels of cholesterol and triglycerides in our blood. And, in turn, those increases can cause arterial blockage or atherosclerosis. Eventually, this also can lead to hardening of the arteries or arteriosclerosis—another dangerous condition that can cause serious problems, including impotence in men and women.

A diet that is high in sodium and fat can contribute to hypertension, which may have to be managed through various medications. I'm sure you remember our earlier discussion of how impotence can be a side effect of those medications, which makes hypertension a double problem.

A diet that is too high in simple carbohydrates, like white breads or bakery products that contain a lot of sugar, can make diabetes more difficult to manage. A poor diet combined with a lack of exercise certainly can contribute to adult-onset, or Type 2, diabetes. And you know that diabetes is a major cause of impotence.

Smoking and drinking alcohol are prominent in the lifestyle of many people, and they both are hazardous to our health and can cause cardiovascular problems that lead to sexual problems. It might be possible to drink in moderation and remain healthy, but there should be no compromise with smoking. Don't do it for a lot of reasons, including the devastating effect it can have on your sex life. (see page 79, Part III.)

Just as inexcusable as smoking is our failure to exercise sufficiently to keep our weight down. Unfortunately, we seem to be breeding couch potatoes by the millions. By the way, that term is in the dictionary, and the definition is not flattering: "A lazy and inactive person, especially one who spends a great deal of time watching television."[42]

The risks are obvious. Lack of exercise leads to being overweight, which can lead to diseases directly linked to impotence—diabetes and hypertension. And failure to exercise is detrimental to the cardiovascular system, which is vital to sexual performance. Need more convincing?

Cigars, overwork, and fried chicken—what an unhealthy combination, and would you believe one of the finest surgeons I know courted disaster with those bad habits. Art worked hard, played hard, and believed his iron constitution would pull him through anything. Shouldn't a doctor know better?

Not this guy. He didn't wake up until his wife—and his body—finally got through to him. The first shock came while he was puffing on a cigar during a break between procedures at the hospital. A dizzy spell led to a nearby bed with worried colleagues racing to control his soaring blood pressure.

After recovering from that setback and being ordered to take a vacation, Art's wife applied the clincher. It wasn't a shape-up-or-ship-out ultimatum, thank heaven, but she made it clear that he had to cut out cigars, alcohol, and his beloved fried chicken or risk losing her as well as his life. She said his Texas-size appetite was killing him, and his disinterest in sex was making her miserable and ruining their marriage.

I wish I could say there was a quick turnaround in this case, but it actually took several years for Art to bring his compulsive ways under control. He needed help and finally got a lot of it—a trainer to monitor an exercise program, a professional dietician to change his eating habits, and a sex therapist to help restore his once-active sex life.

It took time, patience, and love, but Art's eventual turnaround was impressive. Today, his practice is thriving, but more importantly, when I'm around him and his wife, their appreciation for each other is obvious. He finally got the message.

It's all very clear now, isn't it? A healthy lifestyle will protect you against impotence and will contribute to a more active and enjoyable sex life. And if you equate achieving a healthy lifestyle with dietary deprivation and boring, repetitive exercise, think again. Just practice moderation—that's the secret. And I must remind you, your mom was right. Eat a balanced diet in medium amounts, and eat those fruits and vegetables. Exercise daily if you can, but be satisfied with a pleasant walk at your own pace. Now, let's be more specific.

You Need to Know

Exercise improves blood flow to all body parts, including the penis. A regular workout can help prevent impotence.

If you are physically fit, you likely will derive more enjoyment from sex and be more sexually active.

Those who exercise regularly have higher levels of desire, greater sexual confidence, and an increased ability to be aroused and achieve orgasm.

Aerobic exercise triggers the release of endorphins, chemicals produced in the brain that create a sense of well-being and help make you more receptive to sex.

Fitness can boost self-esteem, confidence, and body image, all of which are important factors for positive sexual interaction.

The Proper Diet

■ GETTING STARTED
■ BEYOND THE BASICS
■ NAVIGATING THE RESTAURANT MINEFIELDS

A proper diet is a key component of a healthy style of living. Every day researchers report increasing evidence that what we eat directly affects our health. But "diet" is a word that most of us dread because we associate it with hunger, pain, and sacrifice. And it usually brings to mind another word—"failure." More often than not, we lose weight only to gain it back, which in a lifetime can amount to hundreds of pounds coming and going in a vicious cycle that can kill you.

During many years of talking with doctors, patients, and dieting myself, I've learned three things:

■ People are more likely to stick with a reasonable eating plan if they do it to improve their health or to feel good about themselves rather than having a short-term goal of losing weight.

■ It's easier to maintain a healthy lifestyle if you take it step by step, making gradual but meaningful changes. Again, moderation is the secret.

■ Long-term success is much more likely if you make room for a few treats once in awhile. People don't like to be told that they can never again indulge in their favorite foods.

I encourage you to keep those points in mind as you explore ways to improve your eating habits. If you've been told that you need to lose some weight, I urge you to seek the advice of a registered dietician or a health-care professional. The recommendations I'm offering should be helpful, but you also need to make sure your dietary plan is in keeping with your current level of fitness and health. Guidance from a professional could be very important.

On the other hand, if you are fortunate enough to have only a few pounds to lose, or if you are satisfied with your weight, and you just want to improve your health, then here are three more principles you should find helpful:

Serving sizes—We Americans tend to eat too much—of good things as well as bad. Keep in mind that nutritionists consider serving sizes to be much smaller than you might realize, especially compared with servings in restaurants. For example, it's easier to envision eating eight or nine servings of fruits and vegetables a day when you know that one serving equals one piece of fruit or a half-cup of cooked vegetables. It's also easier to understand cutting back on fatty meats when you know that a protein serving, be it steak, poultry, fish, or tofu, is roughly the size of the palm of a woman's hand.

Small meals—Our meals usually are too big as well. My recommendation is that you eat three small meals and two or three snacks during the day. The result will be that you are less likely to overeat at meal time—and less likely to binge on high-calorie, high-fat snacks.

Variety of foods—If you eat a variety of foods, you'll be more likely to consume all the vitamins, minerals, and phytochemicals (chemicals from plants) a healthy body requires. Also, you'll avoid the boredom that can lead to snacking and bingeing. Of course, we all have favorite foods that we like to fall back on, and there's nothing wrong with that. Just keep in mind that a successful eating plan is an interesting eating plan. Be creative and don't forget that occasional treat.

I assure you it isn't that hard to make substantial improvements in almost any diet—even if you don't like vegetables. Experiment with some foods you haven't tried in a long time. Combined with healthy foods you *do* like, you might change your mind.

The Tomato Solution

But if vegetables remain a tough sell, don't forget the benefits of Italian food. It may surprise you, but foods like spaghetti and pizza could help fight cancer. As it happens, tomato products are rich in a substance called "lycopene," which researchers say may reduce a man's risk of prostate cancer, which of course can cause impotence.

To test this theory, researchers at the Karmanos Cancer Institute in Detroit gave lycopene capsules to men who were about to undergo surgery to remove their cancerous prostate glands.

The study involved thirty-three men who were randomly assigned to take either two, fifteen-milligram capsules of lycopene or nothing for thirty days before their prostate operations.

Before the surgery, the volunteers showed no obvious signs that their cancer had spread. But after the surgery, the doctors found that cancer tissue was less likely to extend all the way to the edges of the lycopene users' prostate glands. And precancerous cells in their prostates were less abnormal looking than those who took a placebo.

Levels of prostate specific antigen (PSA), a measure of tumor activity, also fell 20 percent between the start of treatment and surgery in the lycopene patients. They were unchanged in the comparison group.[43]

"This suggests that lycopene results in a decrease of the tumor size and makes the cancer less aggressive," said Dr. Omar Kucuk, who directed the study.

Eat Your Vegetables

Lycopene belongs to a group of substances called "carotenoids." These are very important to men and women alike. Every day, researchers are discovering new health benefits that they attribute to different carotenoids, some of which may reduce our chances of heart disease and clogged arteries as well as cancer.

Carotenoids are part of the larger group of naturally occurring chemicals called phytochemicals. And that means it is important to eat your vegetables. I realize that many of us don't go for broccoli or Brussels sprouts, but it's a good idea to experiment with cruciferous vegetables to find something you like. This family of vegetables is rich

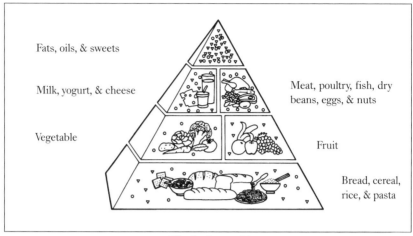

Fats, oils, & sweets

Milk, yogurt, & cheese

Meat, poultry, fish, dry beans, eggs, & nuts

Vegetable

Fruit

Bread, cereal, rice, & pasta

The food pyramid

in beta-carotene, another carotenoid, as well as vitamin C, an important antioxidant. I recommend that you start adding as many dark green and orange vegetables as possible. Sweet potatoes, squash, pumpkin—all of those are high in carotenoids.

And here's a tip for you—try broccoli sprouts. They are even better for you than broccoli itself, and they taste better. Johns Hopkins University School of Medicine researchers discovered that broccoli sprouts contain anywhere from thirty to fifty times the concentration of protective chemicals found in mature broccoli plants.

When you're making a salad, go for the dark lettuces instead of the iceberg. And don't forget fruits. Citrus fruits, berries, melons, tropical fruits—they all have different phytochemicals. If you can include eight or nine servings of fruits and vegetables a day, and if you choose from a variety of your favorites, then you'll be getting all kinds of phytochemicals, not to mention your recommended daily intake of vitamins C, E, and A.

Further support for a healthy diet comes from the respected DASH study, which stands for Dietary Approaches to Stop Hypertension. It found that a combination of eight or nine servings of fruits and vegetables each day, along with three servings of low-fat dairy products, reduced blood pressure as effectively as medication.

GETTING STARTED

Diet is such a hot topic these days, and there are so many books claiming to have all the answers, that it's not hard to become confused. Let me make this as easy as possible. If you're going to make only one change in your eating habits, make it this one: *Cut the fat and replace it with fiber.*

Can one change make that much of a difference? Yes! A healthy eating plan is based on high-fiber foods like fruits, vegetables, and grain products—especially whole grains. Foods that are high in saturated fat are red meats and other fatty meats as well as full-fat dairy products. Foods that are high in trans fats, which are believed to be just as harmful to our cardiovascular health, include many snack chips, fried foods, and margarine—stick margarine being higher in trans fats and tub or liquid margarine being lower.

With that in mind, let's consider a few simple menu ideas that could make a big difference in most people's diets.

Breakfast—Here's a great opportunity to pack a lot of fiber into one relatively low-calorie meal. A bowl of oatmeal or high-fiber cold cereal is a good start. If you're hungry, add a piece of whole-wheat toast with low-fat margarine or jam. Have some skim milk in your coffee and some with your cereal, totaling at least one cup of milk. Top the cereal with a banana or some berries. A half-cup of calcium-fortified orange juice also is a good idea. For variety, have a whole-grain bagel with some low-fat peanut butter or low-fat cream cheese the next day with a half grapefruit or a melon wedge. Keep in mind that with breads, bagels, and all grain products, the whole-grain varieties have much more fiber and other nutrients than those made with white flour.

Lunch—Midday is a good time for a protein boost to get you through the afternoon. Try a lean turkey sandwich on two slices of whole-grain bread with sliced tomatoes. Fill out the meal with vegetables on the side—a small salad of dark lettuce, maybe with some raisins and garbanzo beans, and a vinaigrette-style dressing. Another good option would be a tuna sandwich made with low-fat mayonnaise or yogurt. Or, instead of a sandwich, substitute a meal-size salad made with a lot of different vegetables plus water-packed tuna or a half-cup of beans. If you opt for the salad, add a whole-grain roll. For dessert, have a piece of fruit or some low-fat frozen yogurt. And here's a tip—raspberries, red grapes, figs, and strawberries not only are great for snacks and desserts, they also fight cancer and hypertension.

Dinner—If you're trying to break a steak habit, try substituting salmon or swordfish. These will satisfy almost any meat lover, and they're rich in omega-3 fatty acids, which may reduce the risk of heart disease. On the side have a small salad made with dark greens; a serving or two of vegetables, concentrating on green, red, and orange vegetables; or perhaps some brown-rice pilaf or a baked potato. Use low-fat margarine on the potato and vegetables. Another good menu would be pasta with marinara sauce, which is high in cancer-fighting lycopenes, a small side salad, and maybe some Italian bread. In the sauce, include a variety of vegetables—mushrooms, green peppers, onions, and maybe some white beans or garbanzos.

Snacks—No one likes to feel that they can't eat when the mood strikes. Snacking is a good way to get in some extra nutrients and to stave off the hunger pangs that cause us to binge at meals. Good choices are carrots with a dip made of low-fat yogurt and salsa, a handful of unsalted nuts, a carton of low-fat yogurt, an apple with a piece of cheddar. At night have a glass of skim milk with cookies, if you can afford the calories.

If you follow menu plans like these, then by my count here's what you'll gain: five to ten servings of grains and at least eight servings of fruits and vegetables, which is in keeping with the government's dietary guidelines. Remember, each half bagel, each piece of bread, and every half-cup of pasta counts as one serving, as does each piece of fruit or each half grapefruit, each half-cup of berries or cooked vegetables, and each full cup of dark lettuce greens. Depending on your snacking habits, you can get in even more vegetable servings—with barely any calorie increase. You probably will have a serving of low-fat milk at breakfast, but I suggest trying to add another glass of milk and possibly some low-fat yogurt as the day goes on.

And what do you have to lose? Probably some weight. Let's say you're eating habits are really bad, and you often have bacon and eggs for breakfast, a fast-food burger for lunch, fried chicken and fries for dinner, and potato chips at night. By following my suggestions, you'll be eliminating at least two-thirds of your daily caloric intake, untold grams of fat, and enough sodium that would put you at great risk of hypertension.

Of course, few people are that totally careless about what they eat, but many do rely on fast food for lunch or dinner, or else they indulge in bacon and eggs every day or steak every night. Those habits can be hard to break. That's why it's important to make changes slowly, being sure they become part of a routine before initiating bigger changes.

Also, keep in mind that most people don't have to give up their favorite foods entirely unless they have a serious health condition and are under a doctor's orders to do so. It doesn't take much practice to learn how to make fantastic oven-baked chicken and "fries" as a special weekend treat when there's time to cook. And people who love the taste of meat might find it just as satisfying to use it as a condiment or a flavoring agent in grain and vegetable dishes.

Please remember this. A piece of lean red meat once in a while won't hurt most of us—as long as it's a single serving size, not a giant slab. So weekend barbecues need not become a fond memory—just toss on the chicken and lean meat and skip the high-sodium, high-fat hot dogs.

You Need to Know

Choose foods containing high-fiber, complex carbohydrates, and monounsaturated or polyunsaturated fats instead of refined, low-fiber carbohydrates, and saturated fats.

Read the ingredients on all packaged and canned foods. Some contain more fat, sodium, sugar, and preservatives than you might suspect.

Bake or broil food instead of frying it.

Have a green, leafy salad at least once a day. (Leaf lettuces and spinach are much more nutritious than iceberg lettuce.)

Eat fresh foods instead of canned foods.

Eat more whole-grain products.

Cook vegetables only slightly or eat them raw.

Limit the amount of red meat you consume and eat more fish.

Limit fat, cholesterol, sugar, alcohol, salt, and caffeine.

BEYOND THE BASICS

Most people find that if they consume the recommended numbers of grain, fruit, and vegetable servings, they're less hungry for high-fat, high-sodium foods. In altering their meals this way, they are providing their bodies with plenty of fiber, vitamins, and phytochemicals. By making that switch with your diet, your health will improve measurably.

But there are other foods that are less common in many of our diets—foods that have been proved to have many health benefits already and may have even more as our knowledge increases. And if you like to experiment with new foods, there are many ways to incorporate them into your menus. Here are some suggestions.

Soy protein—Asian populations, whose diets are high in soy protein and low in animal protein, have been shown to have a much lower risk of many conditions that are quite common among Western women: osteoporosis, estrogen-dependent cancers such as uterine cancer, even severe menopause symptoms. Researchers have highlighted a particular class of phytochemicals that is abundant in soy products. These are called "isoflavones," which some experts think could reduce the risk of prostate cancer in men. In addition, regular consumption of soy protein might help reduce blood cholesterol levels. I should add that Asians also consume more vegetables and grains than most Westerners.

And here's something else you should know. Soy foods have what's called "phytoestrogens," which are estrogen-like compounds found in plants. These phytoestrogens may help keep sex hormones in balance along with all the other benefits of soy foods.

Not many Americans have cultivated a taste for tofu and soy milk. But tofu can be made more appetizing if it's used in stir-fries and stews. It also can be blended with other ingredients to make everything from vegetable dips to "cheese" cakes. Some stores now carry flavored tofu that's been treated to give it a firmer, "meatier" texture, which is useful for salads and sandwiches. Also, some vegetable processors are coming out with frozen vegetable blends that include soybeans. As the benefits of soy become better known, I think we can expect even more options.

Olive oil—Mediterranean populations have been shown to have a reduced incidence of heart disease and some cancers. Researchers are attributing this to many factors, one of which is the liberal use of olive oil in place of other types of fats. Olive oil, along with canola oil, is rich in "monounsaturated fats," which are believed to protect against heart disease.

I don't recommend drowning your food in olive oil. But if you like Italian and Greek food, I recommend cooking with olive oil and canola oil instead of other types of fats. Olive oil with red vinegar also makes a tasty salad dressing—much better for you than those creamy, high-fat dressings. Generally, whenever possible, I'd say substitute olive oil or canola oil for other cooking fats.

French researchers, by the way, report that a "Mediterranean" diet, which emphasizes vegetables, fruits, grains, beans, and fish, can decrease the risk of a second heart attack by as much as 70 percent. The results of a four-year study indicate that the Mediterranean population may be relatively protected from coronary heart disease in the first place because of the foods they consume.[44]

Different protein sources—Most Americans have too much protein in their diets, not too little. Excess protein is believed to be a factor in heart disease, so this is something to watch. There are many so-called experts touting high-protein and even high-fat diets, but common sense and sound science don't support their claims.

We all need some protein in our diets, of course. The key is selecting protein sources that offer *maximum* nutritional benefits without contributing too much saturated fat. Making the switch from fatty meats to leaner cuts and substituting fish for meat is the way to go. If you want to add protein sources that pack more fiber, try beans such as white beans, black beans, kidney beans, or garbanzos. Also, give peas and lentils a try. One serving is about a half-cup, which is a good amount for a salad. Soups and stews made with beans, peas, or lentils are welcome meat substitutes in the winter. Every supermarket carries canned beans, which are almost as nutritious as soaking and cooking them from scratch.

If you have trouble digesting beans or, for that matter, all the vegetables you've now added to your diet, there are products on the market that can help. Drinking a big glass of water with each meal also may help—many nutritionists recommend six to eight glasses a day. As with all of these ideas, the best solution is to incorporate them gradually to give your system time to adjust. And don't hesitate to consult with a doctor or a dietician when in doubt.

Let's talk about dieticians for a minute. You need to know how much good they can do either in a group situation or on a personal basis. Pam, who is a perfect example of somebody needing help, was a big woman—too big, in fact. But she always attributed her size to something in her genes. "All of my people are overweight," she used to say. "I eat like everybody else, and I'm still heavy. God meant me to be this way."

Her doctor finally hooked her up with a dietician I know, and Pam learned the awful truth. She was instructed to keep a diary of absolutely *everything* she ate for a week, right down to every Snickers bar she was inhaling between meals and at bedtime. It was a revelation when everything she was consuming was described in detail, and the thousands of calories were counted. Pam was eating enough for two women and weighed just about as much. Some of us need a shock before we act. It worked on Pam.

You Need to Know

You may have noticed that I don't recommend specific calorie or fat intakes in this discussion. Regardless of the national obsession with counting fat grams, I believe that takes the fun out of eating. The meal plans I suggest are flexible enough for most people.

If you need to lose weight, then take out some of the fat, whether it's margarine or butter on your vegetables or oil in your salad dressings. If you happen to be in good health and very active, then you can increase portion sizes to make sure you get enough calories to support your lifestyle.

A healthy diet doesn't require calculators and scales. Nor does it have to mean pain and starvation. As long as you keep things interesting by eating a variety of foods, and as long as you permit yourself the occasional treat, you should be able to make this a life-long habit.

NAVIGATING THE RESTAURANT MINEFIELDS

Dining out—and its modern-day counterpart, carrying out—have become just about as commonplace as cereal for breakfast and barbecue on summer weekends. This relatively recent phenomenon makes sense. People are busier than ever, and they are looking for ways to spend more time with their families—not alone in the kitchen.

Empty nesters with more time on their hands might want to pursue hobbies and entertainment or just relax together. Cooking is not a priority at this stage of life for a lot of people. When we get together with friends or with business acquaintances, more often than not a meal is involved, and dining out allows us to concentrate on each other rather than preparing meals.

This is a dangerous trend in that it is much easier to follow a healthy diet when you prepare your own meals, because you control the portion sizes. You decide what goes on the plate, and you determine how it's made. Therefore, you must learn to protect your health when confronting all those temptations beckoning from a good restaurant menu.

By keeping three points in mind, you easily can anticipate most of the pitfalls.

> Restaurant portions are almost always larger than a serving size as defined by nutrition professionals. Those restaurant bagels? Easily three, even four grain servings. An order of spaghetti and meatballs? Probably about four grain servings and maybe three meat servings—and depending on how much sauce and whether it has any vegetables, maybe only one vegetable serving. Prime rib? Don't ask.

> What you see is not always what you get. Often, foods that appear to be healthy actually are loaded with fat and sodium. Fried chicken or a juicy steak may be self-evident. But did you know that pasta often is tossed with oil? That country-style vegetables are usually swimming in butter? This is fine once in a while, but if you're eating out every night, you might have to ask if your food could be prepared differently.

> Almost every restaurant can accommodate reasonable requests. Even a roadside, budget restaurant can substitute a baked potato or sliced tomatoes for fries. Steakhouse chefs can whip up excellent vegetable plates or pasta dishes. White-tablecloth restaurants usually offer appetizer-size portions of many entrees. This is a safer option than taking part of your food home in a "doggy bag," unless you can get your leftovers refrigerated right away.

Keeping those principles in mind, here are some suggestions and substitutions to guide your restaurant choices.

■ Have a green salad or soup before your entree instead of filling up on bread and butter.

- Choose vinaigrette-style dressings instead of creamy salad dressings.

- Try gazpacho or clear soups instead of cream soups.

- Order lean meats and keep portions small.

- Go for meatless salads or sandwiches, or substitute lean turkey for tuna salad.

- When you are ordering poultry or fish, ask to have it poached or broiled instead of fried.

- Consider appetizers instead of entrees or ask for appetizer-size portions.

- Order your vegetables steamed without cheese or cream sauces. Even if you use butter or margarine on them, you'll be getting less fat.

- Ask for a baked potato instead of fries, and control the amount of butter or margarine you use. In coffee shops, ask for fruit or tomatoes instead of hash browns.

- At the salad bar, load up on dark greens and fresh vegetables. Skip the potato salad, macaroni salad, and other mayonnaise-style salads.

- In Italian restaurants, ask for marinara sauce instead of cream sauces like Alfredo. Ask if the pasta can be made without oil.

- In Chinese restaurants, order stir-fries or steamed vegetables and fish. Skip the fried rice and sweet-and-sour entrees.

- In Japanese restaurants, order sushi instead of tempura. Teriyaki is a low-fat choice although it is high in sodium.

- In Mexican restaurants, order grilled fish, poultry, or vegetables instead of fried foods like tortillas and refried beans. Choose salsa instead of sour cream sauce, and watch those chips!

After you get used to watching your portion sizes and speaking up for yourself, you'll find that making healthy restaurant choices is second nature. Try it! You've got nothing to lose but fat, calories, and sodium. And your sex life should improve.

Choosing Supplements

- Vitamins
- Minerals
- Herbs
- A Word of Caution

We know there are no miracle cures for impotence, but we have found out that a healthy lifestyle can protect us from it and enhance our sex lives in the process. It's also true that there are some dietary supplements that can help ensure that we get the nutrients we need, and some of them can improve our overall sexual health.

If you like to read the labels on food packaging, you are familiar with the term RDA, or Recommended Daily Allowances. The RDAs are established by the National Academy of Sciences, an independent agency chartered by Congress. RDAs are used by nutritionists, dieticians, health-care professionals, and government agencies such as the U.S. Department of Agriculture, which sets national nutrition policy, as well as the U.S. Food and Drug Administration, which regulates food and supplement labeling.

RDAs are developed for healthy men, women, and children. Recently, some of the RDAs have been updated as DRLs—Dietary Reference Intakes. You also might have seen the term "daily value," which is sometimes used as an umbrella term to accommodate these recommendations as they are revisited and updated. There are daily values for many vitamins and minerals but not for other types of supplements such as herbs.

Vitamin and mineral supplements are a hot area of study right now, and it seems that almost every day a new report is published assessing the value of a vitamin or mineral in fighting or preventing disease. Generating the greatest debate are the antioxidant vitamins C, E, and beta-carotene, which the body converts into vitamin A. Some researchers argue that those daily values should be higher than the current recommendations for healthy people. Others counter that the evidence doesn't support high doses, and that high doses instead may be harmful.

Understandably, many people don't know how much of all these different nutrients they should be getting. And as a doctor, I find it difficult to make a blanket recommendation. But there are a few key vitamins and minerals that I believe are essential to our cardiovascular health—and to proper sexual functioning. Let's explore a few supplements here, but I encourage you to do some further research and to consult with your doctor.

Vitamins

One of the trendiest categories of dietary supplements these days involves antioxidant vitamins. And this is one case where the publicity is well deserved. Here's how antioxidants work. We all have a certain number of molecules called "free radicals" in our bodies. A free radical is an oxygen molecule that's missing an electron—so the danger is that the free radical will bind to something and may cause harm. For example, if the free radical binds itself to our DNA, it can cause cancer. If it hooks onto a fatty acid, it can contribute to the formation of plaque in our bloodstream, which could then form the clots that lead to heart attack or stroke—or possibly impotence.

Antioxidants benefit us by removing free radicals from the body. When we have enough antioxidants in our bodies to remove these free radicals, our systems have a better chance of resisting them. That's why, for some people, I recommend supplemental vitamin C, vitamin E, and beta-carotene, which we have noted the body converts into vitamin A.

Realistically speaking, most people do not get enough antioxidants from their diets. Green, orange, and red vegetables and fruits are great sources of all these vitamins, but most people just don't eat enough of them. I recommend eight or nine servings of fruits and vegetables every day, and most of us don't consume anywhere near that much.

Having said that, I want to point out that it is possible to get too much of a good thing—including vitamins. There are many people who assume that if something is good for them, then they should take it in unlimited amounts. That's a mistake. It's very important not to overdose.

For example, some people already may be taking a multivitamin that's high in antioxidant vitamins, and they also may consume a lot of fruits and vegetables. These people probably don't need antioxidant supplements, but usually I've found that those who don't like vegetables probably can benefit from a supplement.

We should get at least the recommended daily value for every vitamin and mineral, and in some cases maybe more if our doctor thinks it's advisable. I believe it's especially important to take in enough of the antioxidant vitamins, either in our diet or through supplements. My concern is that most people are getting too few of them, not too many.

Vitamin E—This is one antioxidant vitamin that's hard to overdose on from dietary sources—in fact, it's hard to consume enough without a supplement, and there is some evidence that doses above the recommended daily value protect against heart attack. There's also increasing evidence that vitamin E can help protect against cancer, and the National Cancer Institute is conducting clinical trials that should provide further understanding. In the meantime, patients who are at risk for these conditions should talk with their doctors about taking supplemental vitamin E.

Cancer researchers have produced studies giving high vitamin E intake credit for lower rates of lung, colon, and cervical cancers, and a reduced risk of cardiovascular disease. It may help prevent atherosclerosis, and it might help improve insulin regulation and reduce blood glucose levels in diabetics. Evidence also is surfacing that vitamin E could improve the immune response in older adults. And, of particular interest to men, it also might reduce the risk of prostate cancer.

The daily value for adult men and women is twelve to fifteen IU (International Units), or eight to ten milligrams. Some health groups recommend daily intakes of one hundred to four hundred IU or even higher.

It is difficult to get Vitamin E from foods. In fact, polyunsaturated vegetable oils like safflower oil are among the best dietary sources—but to rely on these for our vitamin E consumption would cause a significant increase in our fat and calorie intake. Avocados, nuts, whole grains, wheat germ, and some green leafy vegetables are other good sources. Liver and margarine are high in vitamin E. But anyone interested in taking in more than the daily value for vitamin E should consider a supplement since it is not especially common in heart-healthy foods.

Vitamin C—This vitamin has been credited with curing everything from cancer to the common cold, but it really isn't a cure for anything. However, it does seem to have a protective effect against an array of health conditions. It is a known antioxidant against cancer cells, may reduce the risk of death from cardiovascular disease, and it might help improve insulin regulation in diabetics. High doses of vitamin C are routinely recommended for smokers and for those who are subject to secondhand smoke.

The daily value for most adults is only sixty milligrams, but many researchers and health-care professionals recommend higher doses. You might be getting enough if you eat a lot of fruits and vegetables. Good sources of vitamin C are citrus fruits, tomatoes, cantaloupe, green peppers, cruciferous vegetables like broccoli, and dark greens.

Vitamin D—I mention vitamin D here for both women and men not because it's specifically relevant to cardiovascular or sexual health, but because our bodies must have it to ensure that enough calcium is deposited in our bones. Recently, the National Academy of Sciences issued new recommendations for vitamin D, and they're the same for men and women: ages fifty and younger, two hundred IU; ages fifty-one to seventy, four hundred IU; and seventy-one and older, six hundred IU.

Fish, especially oily fish, have some vitamin D, and milk usually is fortified with vitamin D. Sunshine helps our bodies synthesize vitamin D, but since sunscreens have become second nature for many people, that's not much help. Most multivitamins and many calcium supplements include vitamin D. Since most people don't drink three glasses of fortified milk every day, I recommend you check the vitamin D content of your multivitamin.

Beta-carotene—Beta-carotene and other carotenoids are the subject of intense research for their potential ability to reduce the risk of many types of cancer, including lung, liver, stomach, colon, and numerous others.

There are no RDAs or daily values for any of the carotenoids. But they are believed to be safe even at relatively high levels for most people. This makes beta-carotene especially valuable as an alternative to vitamin A since the body turns it into that vitamin anyway. (An important antioxidant itself, vitamin A is thought to be toxic at very high levels.)

Good sources of beta-carotene include orange and green fruits and vegetables. The list, which is quite long, includes carrots, sweet potatoes, winter squashes, cruciferous vegetables such as broccoli, green leafy vegetables such as spinach or kale, peas, peppers, cantaloupe, apricots, and peaches. If you eat a variety of fruits and vegetables, you should be taking in enough beta-carotene. But I think that many men and women could benefit from a supplement that includes both beta-carotene and vitamin E.

The B vitamins—There are several important B vitamins, and our bodies require all of them. Deficiencies in these important nutrients were very common at one time but less so today. Now, a varied diet provides most people with enough of the B vitamins, especially if it's supplemented with a good multivitamin.

The most important newsmaker on the B vitamin scene these days is folic acid. The daily value for pregnant women is four hundred micrograms, but most health organizations and the government recommend that all women of childbearing age consume that much. The reason is that folic acid is very important in preventing birth defects. However, the latest research shows that there's another reason for both men and women to take in four hundred micrograms: Folic acid seems to reduce the risk of heart disease and stroke, apparently by reducing the levels of homocysteine in the blood. Also, B_6 and B_{12} may play a lesser role.

As mandated by the FDA, bread, cereal, and grain products now have to be fortified with folic acid, and all of those are important components of a healthy diet. But I recommend that you make sure your multivitamin contains four hundred micrograms. It also should round out your intake of all the B vitamins. You should talk to your doctor about a B-complex formula, especially if you are older. Too much folic acid can mask a B_{12} deficiency, which is common in older people, but this can be corrected by taking a balanced supplement.

MINERALS

There are numerous macrominerals and trace minerals in our diet, several of which have RDAs. All are essential to the proper functioning of our musculoskeletal, cardiovascular, and nervous systems. A balanced diet that includes several whole-grain servings a day along with low-fat dairy products, supplemented by a good multiformula, should ensure that most people get the necessary amounts of minerals. However, there are a few minerals that I want to discuss individually:

Calcium—Everyone at one time was concerned about "iron-poor blood"—getting enough iron into our diets. Now, the concern has shifted to calcium, and with good reason. Calcium is essential in preventing osteoporosis in men as well as women. It also seems to protect against hypertension, and research is continuing in other areas. By the way, osteoporosis is much more prevalent in men than most of us realize. It is estimated that 25 million Americans have osteoporosis, and 20 percent of them are men.[45]

Our bone density stops building by the age of twenty, and as early as our thirties, it starts to decrease. The latest research shows that if we didn't get a lot of calcium as children, then there's not much we can do as adults to make up for it in terms of building bone density. To stave off the loss of bone density we can get plenty of weight-bearing exercise, and we can ensure that we take in enough calcium. But that's not easy to do.

Calcium is difficult to get from dietary sources, especially for people who don't like or tolerate milk. And it's almost impossible to get enough calcium in a multivitamin. Clearly, calcium is an exception to my earlier statement that we can get most of our minerals from one good supplement. The daily value for most women—and for men over fifty—is twelve hundred milligrams. Some researchers recommend a daily intake of as much as fifteen hundred milligrams.

Dietary sources such as low-fat dairy products are very efficient delivery systems. My advice is to take an honest look at how much calcium you consume in your diet and then supplement the rest. If you have a glass of skim milk and a carton of yogurt every day, you may need only another three hundred to six hundred milligrams. If you depend entirely on supplements, you may need to take a couple of those. Here's a tip. If you're taking more than one calcium supplement a day, try to stagger them. You'll get better absorption that way. And don't forget the vitamin D—or even boron and magnesium.

Zinc—As I said earlier, all of the minerals are so important that I hesitate to emphasize one over the others. But I mention zinc here for two reasons: First, the latest research shows that zinc may help prevent atherosclerosis and boost our immune function. Second, researchers claim that zinc can relieve prostate symptoms.

Some of us don't get enough zinc in our diets and need to do something about it. Meat and seafood are good sources of zinc, but for those who are reducing their meat consumption, whole grains and legumes also are good sources. Many supplements provide 100 percent of the daily value for zinc. The RDA is only twelve milligrams for women and fifteen for men, and your doctor can tell you if you need more. Keep in mind that it's important not to take excessive amounts of calcium, which may block zinc absorption.

Selenium—I mention selenium because recent research has shown that it may have an antioxidant function against cancer cells, and that it might help protect against cancer in other ways. Studies have shown that selenium also may reduce the risk of cardiovascular disease and improve immune functioning.

The media is quick to report these studies, and understandably so. But keep in mind that high-dosage selenium supplementation not only is premature, it can be toxic. Instead, make sure your supplement contains the daily value—fifty-five micrograms for most women, and seventy for men—especially if you don't eat a lot of whole-grain products such as brown rice and whole wheat, meat, or fish.

Iron—It is the most abundant element on earth and is an essential trace mineral for humans. Its use for therapeutic effect goes back thousands of years. The Greeks recommended iron in wine as a way to restore male potency, and the Egyptians thought it was a cure for baldness. Two-thirds of iron contained in the body is present in blood. The rest is stored in the liver, spleen, bone marrow, and muscles.

A National Institute of Aging study suggests that low iron levels are linked to an increased likelihood of death in elderly people. Researchers found that men with the highest iron levels had only 20 percent of the risk of dying of heart disease than those with the lowest levels. Women with the highest levels were about half as likely to die of heart disease compared to those with the lowest levels.

Other research has linked *high* iron levels with an increased risk of heart disease. Hemochromatosis refers to iron overload disorders, which might be hereditary and may affect as many as one in two hundred people according to some experts. Therapy involves repeated bleeding to remove excess iron or a diet rich in bread, cereals, fruits, and vegetables. If you have any concerns about iron, consult with your doctor.

HERBS

Vitamins and minerals contribute greatly to our well-being, but there are other types of dietary supplements that are receiving increased public attention these days. Herbs especially have leaped to the forefront as "natural remedies" for all sorts of health problems, including sexual.

But let me caution you, some popular "natural remedies" are more credible than others are. For example, a much better case can be made for herbs like ginseng or ginkgo biloba than, say, Spanish fly, which was one of the more memorable frauds of the seventies.

The Chinese have used ginseng for centuries, and it's gaining notice in the West as a booster of energy and libido. Ginkgo biloba is widely used in Europe as well as Asia, and is believed to improve memory and mental ability as well as being used as an anticoagulant or even an antioxidant.

Those two herbs, and some others, probably are effective to a certain extent and safe to use in moderate doses. But I would recommend that anyone who wants to try them consult with a doctor first to make sure there won't be a risk of drug interaction. If patients want to try some of these herbs, it is important that their physician take a detailed history of any other drugs they might be using.

Keep in mind that herbs are not subject to the same regulations as drugs. They're not tested for effectiveness, and they often don't list specific conditions and dosages on the label—so it's hard for people to tell how much to take and which herbs might help. You need to be a good label reader.

Also, some herbs are simply ineffective while others are serious medicine—so it's important to check with a doctor before taking an herbal remedy. I don't see any harm in some of these products as long as people use common sense. However, I would not want someone to count on them as a cure for impotence. Some herbs may boost your energy level or even your libido—but that's about it.

One herb that people have been focusing on lately is saw palmetto. This herb is certainly no answer for impotence or prostate cancer, but it does seem to have a beneficial effect on prostate function. Saw palmetto has become one of the best-selling herbal remedies in the United States and Europe, and it often is prescribed in Germany for a condition called BPH, or benign prostatic hyperplasia (an enlarged prostate). Men who have this condition often have urinary problems and general discomfort, which certainly can affect their sex drive. In the United States, this condition is treated with prescription drugs.

Top Ten Herbs You Can Trust

According to the editors of the newsletter "Environmental Nutrition,"[46] scientific evidence supports the safety and effectiveness of these ten herbs:

Bilberry	Ginkgo	St. John's Wort
Echinacea	Hawthorn	Valerian
Feverfew	Milk Thistle	Ginger
	Saw Palmetto	

Top 20 Herbs You Can't Trust

On the other hand, editors of "Environmental Nutrition" have named these herbs as unsafe or too easily misused and say they are best avoided:

Aconite	Foxglove	Pennyroyal
Belladonna	Germander	Poke
Broom	Jin bu huan	Rue
Chaparral	Liferoot	Sassafras
Coltsfoot	Lily of the Valley	Skullcap
Comfrey	Mandrake	Wormwood
Ephedra	Mistletoe	

A WORD OF CAUTION

Another category of "natural remedies" that is receiving increased attention is hormones—specifically DHEA. The body converts this hormone into the sex hormones estrogen and testosterone. DHEA actually has been around for a long time, having been studied for years by scientists as a possible treatment for cancer, heart disease, aging, and impotence.

The theory is that since our levels of DHEA begin to drop during our teenage years and continue to decline throughout our adult lives, we can slow the aging process by replenishing our levels of the hormone. But regardless of the claims that some people have been making, no connection has been established so far in humans.

Also, like herbal products, these "natural hormones" are not subject to the same safety and efficacy regulations as drugs. So in my opinion, even though some of these so-called "natural hormones" may be cheaper than the treatments we've talked about, you'd be wasting your money.

I'm not saying there never will be a low-cost remedy for impotence that you can pick up at the store. I'm just saying that in most cases you won't get the results you want, and there is the possibility that you could get hurt. Just because a treatment is considered "natural" doesn't mean it isn't dangerous.

There is so much interest in the subject of impotence, and people are so anxious for a cure, that a lot of unscrupulous marketers have been pushing "solutions" that are out-and-out fraudulent. You may have seen some of these advertised in the backs of magazines, or you may have received solicitations in the mail. If you look carefully, you'll see a lot of suggestive pictures and a lot of dramatic claims—but what you won't find are specific medical credentials. Unfortunately, many men and women are taken in by these claims because they're so desperate for help.

There are many vitamins, minerals, and herbs that can improve our health and maybe our energy levels. But when it comes to diagnosing and treating impotence, we need to see a doctor. Only then can people start making the decisions about which treatment is best for them, and what kind of help they need to regain their sexual and emotional intimacy. And never underestimate the power of a healthy lifestyle in achieving and maintaining optimal sexual health.

You Need to Know

Proteins form the basic structure of body tissue and organs. The body uses proteins for growth and repair of cells. Proteins are found in eggs, milk, cheese, tofu, nuts, meat, fish, poultry, dried beans, split peas, and lentils.

Carbohydrates are the body's main source of energy. They are found in potatoes, bread, cereals, grains, pasta, milk, yogurt, vegetables, and fruit.

Fats provide energy and are used for growth and repair of tissues. They are found in olives, nuts, cheese, meat, fish, poultry, butter, oils, avocados, and mayonnaise.

Fiber is found in plants and is not digested by the body. It provides what is considered "bulk," which is used by the large intestine to help remove waste through bowel movements.

Vitamins are complex chemicals that help to regulate metabolism and help the brain, nerves, muscles, skin, and bones function properly.

Minerals are necessary for the body to function properly. Calcium is necessary for healthy teeth and bones, and zinc and magnesium are needed to control cell metabolism. Vitamins and minerals are found in many foods, especially milk, cheese, green leafy vegetables, fish, meat, and poultry.[47]

The Importance of Exercise

- JUST SAY YES!
- DEVISING A PLAN
- THE LAST WORD

After all these years, I am still amazed by how resilient the human spirit can be. Gary is a perfect example of what I'm talking about. Today he nonchalantly describes the "episode" that nearly took his life five years ago, but he is almost boastful in recounting how he bounced back from that severe heart attack.

He decided that exercise would be his salvation, and it has been, thanks to his determination and a carefully supervised program. Proper diet and excellent medical care also contributed to his recovery, but he gives much of the credit to his commitment to some form of physical activity every day, including tennis and brisk walking.

In one of the most significant medical breakthroughs in recent memory, a San Francisco doctor, Dean Ornish, showed that moderate exercise combined with a diet that was very low in fat reduced and even reversed arterial blockage, or atherosclerosis, in heart attack victims. Gary is a perfect example.

For all of us, the evidence is overwhelming that exercise will improve our overall health as well as ward off illnesses that we are bound to confront in our lifetimes. In fact, it is so clearly beneficial that I am continually amazed that many Americans remain reluctant to break a sweat.

Let's look at some specific reasons why you should exercise with the hope that the facts will inspire you to make a healthy decision concerning your future.

You Need to Know

Regular exercise helps maintain a healthy weight, which prevents diseases directly linked to impotence—diabetes and hypertension, for example.

Exercise improves your cardiovascular health and reduces your blood cholesterol levels. Both of these are very important in preventing impotence as well as in helping those who already are experiencing the problem.

A regular exercise program can elevate your spirits, which is going to contribute to your enjoyment of sex.

Exercise and diet are the only proven ways to maintain weight loss. Combined with diet, it's the best weapon we have against cardiovascular disease and hypertension. Exercise boosts our immune response and improves state of mind. It reduces our triglyceride levels where diet alone doesn't work, and it helps regulate blood glucose levels in diabetics. It also strengthens our muscles and our endurance.

Which brings me to the most important muscle of all—your heart. If you don't exercise it often gets weak, and that does not bode well for your sex life. Unfortunately, our daily routines usually involve nothing more than sitting or standing much of the time. Our hearts weren't designed for such inactivity, and the result is less efficiency for all of our muscles if we don't do something about it.

When you exert yourself, your heart beats faster to produce more oxygen, which is carried by the blood to your muscles. And if you exercise regularly, your muscles use oxygen more efficiently, your heart pumps more blood with each beat, and it doesn't have to work as hard.

Routine, daily life is much less tiring if your heart is trained and efficient, and any strenuous activities can be accomplished with much less effort and for a longer period of time. Many types of exercise are good for your heart, which is so important for general health and fitness, especially as you get older.

JUST SAY YES!

I believe the key to starting an exercise program and sticking with it is very simple. Find an activity you enjoy, something that is more of a game than a tedious workout, something that makes your competitive juices flow a bit. I usually advise my patients to try a number of activities before making a routine of anything. Just like with your diet, variety and moderation are the keys to a successful exercise program. But I understand that it's difficult to get started, which is why I have included some suggestions.

Decide on a couple of activities that sound appealing and allot an average of thirty minutes a day to them. One day it may be an hour, the next day you might take off. But strive for thirty minutes a day for as many days a week as you can. If you find the right mix of activities, you also might find yourself making even more time for them.

Just as there are food groups that we should include in planning our daily menus, there are different forms of exercise that should be included in planning a fitness "menu."

Aerobic exercise—As most people know by now, aerobic exercise strengthens the heart and lungs by making them work harder to deliver oxygen to the rest of the body. If you haven't set foot in a gym or health club in years, and you don't remember those days very fondly, don't despair. There are plenty of other activities that are both aerobic and fun such as dancing, walking, jogging, swimming, bicycle riding, and many more. If you *do* like the camaraderie of a gym or health club, or you believe you need more structure, there are facilities that accommodate all age groups and fitness levels. Just make an appointment with the director and ask for a tour. You'll be glad you got started!

Here are some tips if you take up walking for aerobic exercise: Walk briskly enough to deepen your breathing comfortably and increase your heart rate.

▪ Assume a tall posture, head up with shoulders back and abdomen in.

▪ Land on the heel of your foot. Roll forward onto the ball of your foot, then push off from your toes.

▪ Take even, comfortable strides.

▪ Allow your arms to swing freely and rhythmically.

Strength training—Strength training may bring to mind unwelcome images of muscle-bound bodybuilders, but that's not what I have in mind here. Exercises that are specifically designed to improve muscle tone, strengthen the bones, and increase muscle mass don't have to make you look like a bulked-up football player. If you join a gym or health club, you can have a trainer develop a program to meet your unique needs. If you don't, you can use free weights, rubber bands, and exercise videos to develop your own twenty-minute or half-hour routine at home.

Try these simple strengthening exercises:

▪ **Finger squeeze**—Straighten arms in front at shoulder level, palms down. Make a fist, then release. Turn palms up, make a fist, and release.

▪ **Arm circles**—Start with arms straight out to the side at shoulder level. Rotate arms from shoulders forward, then backward.

▪ **Shoulder shrug**—Lift shoulders up toward your ears, then back, down, and relax.

▪ **Leg flexion**—Stand erect, holding onto a chair or table for support. Lift one leg forward, then back from the hip. Be careful not to lean forward and back.

■ **Leg extension**—Sitting in a chair, back straight, knees bent, and feet flat on the floor, tighten knee and raise foot up. Alternate with each leg.

■ **Calf raises**—Hold onto something for support if you like. Raise up on your toes, lifting heels. Slowly lower yourself back down to your heels.

■ **Squat**—Start with feet shoulder-width apart. Hold onto the back of a chair for support. Keep back straight and slowly bend knees as if you are going to sit. Slowly return to start position. Do not go down too far! This will improve as you get stronger.

■ **Toe raises**—Standing or sitting with feet shoulder-width apart, raise your toes off the floor as if tapping to music.

■ **Abdominal strengthening**—Stand or sit straight. Take a deep breath in through your nose, then slowly exhale through your mouth as if blowing out a candle. Feel your stomach go in as you blow out. Hold stomach tight after blowing out, then relax and repeat.

■ **Sit-up**—Lay on the floor with your knees bent and feet flat. Reach with your arms toward your knees, raising your head and shoulders off the floor. You should readily feel your stomach muscles tighten. Slowly return head and shoulders to the floor. Work up to doing five to ten repetitions.[48]

Flexibility exercises—These exercises are designed to make you more limber and flexible, which will have the immediate result of protecting you from injury during your other workouts. A longer-term benefit may be that as you age you'll be less likely to fall and suffer a severe break or fracture. Many quality exercise videos include flexibility exercises along with aerobics and strength training. Familiar moves like the cat-and-camel stretch, the side bend, and others also improve your flexibility. You can build some stretches right into your other workouts. For example, stretch a few minutes before your walk or before your weight session, and then do a few more stretches to cool down. Yoga is a great way to stretch—and it also improves muscle tone at the same time.

Here are some flexibility exercises:

- **Neck circles**—Standing or sitting in a chair, slowly move chin over to one shoulder and then to the other as if nodding "no." Slowly lift your chin up slightly and back down toward your chest as if nodding "yes." Repeat several times.

- **Flexed leg back stretch**—Stand with knees slightly bent and feet shoulder-width apart. Slowly and gently slide hands down front of legs, bringing fingertips toward the floor. You should feel a stretch in the back of your legs. Hold for the count of five when you start to feel the stretch.

- **Side bends**—Stand with feet shoulder-width apart. Slide right hand down right leg toward knee. Repeat to left side. Hold five seconds, five repetitions to each side.

- **Overhead reach**—Take in a deep breath as you raise your arms overhead. Exhale slowly as you lower your arms behind your head or to your shoulders, then return to your sides.

- **Shin and quadriceps stretch**—Kneel on both knees, turn to right and press down on right ankle with right hand and hold. Keep hips thrust forward. Do not sit on heels. Repeat on left side.

- **Hip and thigh stretch**—Kneel with right knee directly above right ankle and stretch left leg backward so knee touches floor. Place hands on floor or seat of chair for balance.[49]

DEVISING A PLAN

First, ask yourself these questions:

> Are there any sports that you really enjoy? Or are there certain physical activities that you've abandoned because you're too busy?

> When it comes to exercising, do you prefer the privacy of your home? If so, can you clear an area near a television set for a rollaway exercise mat and reserve some time with the family VCR?

Do you prefer the structure and the camaraderie of a gym or health club? Do you have a membership that you're not using, or have you explored local clubs that cater to your lifestyle and age group?

Are you an early bird? Can you bring yourself to rise earlier in the morning three times a week for a half-hour walk?

Do you have the budget and the space to install some home gym equipment such as a treadmill or a stationary bike? Do you have a pool, and do you use it?

After you've given those questions some thought, it's time to custom-design your program. Remember to take it easy at first, especially if you haven't exercised in a while.

Here are a few examples of programs that work:

Plan A—Two or three mornings or evenings a week, take a brisk, half-hour walk. (Stretch first!) Twice a week, work out with a home exercise video for strength and flexibility. Twice a week, work with a trainer at a gym. On Saturday or Sunday, swim laps and then relax by the pool if one is available.

Plan B—Twice a week, work out on a treadmill. (Stretch first!) Twice a week, do a strength-training video. Once a week, attend a yoga class or golf with your spouse or friends. On Saturday or Sunday, take an hour-long walk, preferably with someone.

Plan C—Twice a week, attend a dance class or work out on the treadmill or jog with someone. (Stretch first!) Twice a week, do a strength-training video. Twice a week, swim laps. On Saturday or Sunday, take a long bike ride.

You may have noticed three things about these suggestions. First, each plan includes aerobic, strength training, and, if you include your stretches, flexibility exercises. Second, each plan includes some weight-bearing exercise, which is essential to maintaining bone mass. I don't recommend relying on swimming or bike riding as your only aerobic exercise. You also should include walking or dancing. Third, each plan becomes progressively more time consuming. That's because once you start, you'll find it easier to make the time, and you'll miss it if you don't. On the other hand, you can start off even slower: a thirty-minute walk twice a week and the video only once. My point is that once you get started you'll begin to emphasize the activities you like the most.

You Need to Know

Regular physical activity lowers blood pressure and prevents the development of high blood pressure.

Someone who is very inactive has six times the risk of heart disease as someone who is active.

Those who exercise can expect to have a 24 percent drop in blood levels of cholesterol and a 10 percent drop in low-density lipoprotein, the "bad" cholesterol.

Physical activity also benefits the blood-clotting system, reducing the body's ability to produce dangerous blood clots that can cause heart attack or stroke.

Physical activity improves the ability of endothelial cells that line blood vessels to produce nitric oxide, which causes blood vessels to relax and contract more efficiently.

THE LAST WORD

Programs like the ones we've outlined will improve your health, your sense of well-being, and will help combat impotence as well as other sexual problems. But there is another more subtle form of exercise that I want you to know about. You may have heard of Kegel exercises, and possibly you have tried them at one time. These exercises often are prescribed for women, especially those experiencing some urinary incontinence. But I would like to recommend them for both men and women in order to help everyone strengthen muscles in the pelvic area.

These exercises can be done anytime, anywhere, so there's no good reason not to get started. To perform Kegel exercises, you simply contract the muscle you use when you're trying to stop the flow of urine. At the same time, tense the same muscle you would use if you were trying to stop a bowel movement. Hold the position for ten seconds, then relax. Do this thirty times or more, depending on your doctor's recommendation.

Also, I recommend another series of pelvic exercises, which simply amounts to contracting your pelvic area upward and forward from a seated position. This is best done if you're alone in your office, watching television, or traveling in the car. If you're using public transportation, you might receive some questioning glances, so don't get carried away.

I hope you now are convinced that you can start an exercise program even if you haven't been active in years. But if you have been inactive, please check with your doctor before beginning any program. A stress test could be in order, especially if you are older; if you've been diagnosed with cardiovascular disease, hypertension, diabetes, or other diseases; or if you haven't been checked in a while. If your doctor recommends a stress test, please take that as an order and not a suggestion.

Finally, I understand that there are some people who simply have an aversion to almost any form of working out. Strenuous exercise of any kind is the last thing they want to do. But those reluctant souls want to be healthy just like the rest of us, so I have some good news for them.

University of Washington research suggests that walking or gardening for merely an hour a week will lower heart attack risk significantly. The study examined the activities of both heart-attack patients and healthy people. Compared with those who don't exercise at all, people who at least walk regularly can reduce the risk of cardiac arrest 73 percent. Those who garden regularly can lower the risk by 66 percent.[50]

That should convince you that you need to exercise, even moderately. So take the plunge. I guarantee that your health will improve, your outlook will brighten, and your ability to enjoy an intimate relationship will be enhanced. No excuses, now. Get a move on and exercise your way to a better sex life and improved health.

Afterword

Bringing life to an idea I had several years ago has had a surprising side benefit. In many ways, assembling information for this book has been a sentimental journey, rewarding me with images of almost forgotten faces, stirring memories of the highlights of a rewarding career. One of the most poignant of those reflections comes from my first days as a physician. There was a rush of joy when I realized that I had the ability to help people maintain their health and sense of well-being. And seeing a baby come into this world always has been absolutely thrilling to me.

I won't diminish the value of those memories by telling you that publishing *Putting Impotence to Bed* has given me a similar thrill, but the pleasure I'm feeling as we conclude this project has a familiar tingle. Knowledge is the best antidote for our repressed sexuality and ignorance of our marvelous bodies, and I am experiencing a sense of satisfaction as I contemplate our contribution to the understanding of a subject that has been in the shadows for too long.

A surgeon can't perform at his best without competent support, and the same can be said for writing a book. A strong sense of teamwork and a singleness of purpose has produced what I hope has been an enlightening experience for those who have digested the facts of our presentation. Our aim from the start has been to explore the cutting edge of research and to impart the most current wisdom in a straightforward way. If we have succeeded, credit must go to the dedicated group that has been instrumental in bringing my original idea to fruition.

I also complete this effort with some apprehension, because the scientific understanding of sexual dysfunction is expanding so rapidly that the general public might not be able to keep pace. Therefore, I close with this essential advice—do not let up in your search for the truth about your sexuality and its vital role in a fulfilling life. We still have a lot to learn about ourselves.

Joseph L. Godat, M.D.

Endnotes

Part I

1   This is the hotel where John Belushi died of a drug overdose and where Leonardo DiCaprio, who reportedly is a smoker, often stays.

2   E. Laumann, J. Gagnon, R. Michael, and S. Michaels, *The Social Organization of Sexuality: Sexual Practices in the United States* (Chicago: University of Chicago Press 1994).

3   The last three items were asked only of respondents who were sexually active during the previous twelve-month period.

4   Sources: *The Journal of the American Medical Association* and *Newsweek* magazine.

5   The research was conducted by a team led by Dr. Jonathan L. Tilly at Massachusetts General Hospital's Vincent Center for Reproductive Biology in Boston.

6   The study's primary author was Dr. Glenn Braunstein of Cedars-Sinai Medical Center in Los Angeles. His study, released June 15, 1999, involved fifty-seven women over a nine-month period. He said that the next step is a broader study involving more women over a longer period of time.

7   Robert Crooks, Karla Baur, *Our Sexuality, Sixth Edition* (Brooks/Cole Publishing Company, Pacific Grove, CA., 1996), pp. 459–460. The authors offer some excellent advice under the heading "Some Helpful Strategies for Delaying Ejaculation." It

also is good advice for men who have no problem but who want to enhance their sexual pleasure. Seeing a sex therapist is recommended if the problem persists.

8   This was the finding of the highly regarded DASH study. DASH stands for Dietary Approaches to Stop Hypertension.

Part II

9   Robert Crooks, Karla Baur, *Our Sexuality, Sixth Edition* (Brooks/Cole Publishing Company, Pacific Grove, CA., 1996). I highly recommend this informative book because of its thoroughness and clarity of thought. All men and women interested in various aspects of their sexuality should read and rely on this text. I made extensive use of *Our Sexuality* as a resource in doing this particular section, and have relied on its definitions because they are so concise and devoid of complicated medical terminology.

10   I believe O'Connell's research succeeded because she dissected the cadavers of young females. Previous dissections have been done on older women whose clitoral tissue had shrunk.

11   Susan Williamson and Rachel Nowak, *New Scientist*, August 1, 1998. Glennda Chui, *San Jose Mercury News*, July 29, 1998.

12   Lawrence K. Altman, *The New York Times*, June 16, 1999, p. A21.

13   Source: Women's Cancer Network.

14   William Masters and Virginia Johnson were the authors of the groundbreaking book *Human Sexual Response*. (Boston, Little, Brown, 1966.) Their work is a major contribution to understanding the physiology of human sexual response. It's very technical, but for those who want more detailed information, it is a good source.

15   We refer to a number of actual case studies in this text, but we have used fictitious names and have altered a few details to protect the privacy of patients.

16   Source: American Heart Association.

17   Gail Sheehy, *The Silent Passage*, (Random House, New York, 1991.)

18   B. Starr, and M. Weiner, *The Starr Weiner Report on Sex and Sexuality in the Mature Years* (New York: Stein & Day, 1981).

Part III

19   David R. Reuben, *Everything You Always Wanted to Know About Sex but Were Afraid to Ask* (New York: David McKay, 1969), pp. 98–99.

20   Donald F. Tapley et al. *The Columbia University College of Physicians and Surgeons Complete Home Medical Guide,* rev. ed. (New York: Crown, 1989) p. 181.

21   Simeon Margolis and Hamilton Moses III, *The Johns Hopkins Medical Handbook* (New York: Rebus, 1992), p. 396.

22   Source: National Institute of Diabetes and Digestive and Kidney Diseases.

23   Source: American Diabetes Association.

24   American Diabetes Association, *Clinical Diabetes*, July 1998.

25   Source: American Diabetes Association.

26   Mike Wallace, *60 Minutes*, CBS, November 8, 1998.

27   Source: The American Lung Association.

28   Source: National Institute on Alcohol Abuse and Alcoholism.

29   Source: American Cancer Society.

30   Joe Kita, "The Unseen Danger," *Bicycling* magazine, August 1997.

31   Steven Morganstern, M.D., Allen Abrahams, Ph.D., *Overcoming Impotence* (New Jersey: Prentice Hall, 1994), p. 104.

32   Source: The National Institutes of Health.

33   Sources: *Drug Facts and Comparisons*, 1998. Facts and Comparisons, St. Louis. Yudofsky, Stuard, M.D., Robert Hales, M.D., and Tom Ferguson, M.D., *What You Need to Know About Psychiatric Drugs.* (Grove Widenfield, N.Y., 1991). *American Journal of Psychiatry*. National Institutes of Health. American Psychiatric Association.

Part IV

34   Source: Pfizer Inc.

35   Associated Press report, March 7, 1999.

36   Larry Tye, the *Boston Globe*, October 23, 1998.

37   Source: Food and Drug Administration.

38   *Dateline NBC*, November 1998.

39   Source: Medical Tribune News Service.

40   Osbon Medical Systems offers a twenty-four-hour help line, 1–800–438–8592.

41   David France, *The New York Times*, February 17, 1999.

Part V

42   Source: *Merriam Webster's Collegiate Dictionary*, Tenth Edition.

43   The findings were presented at a meeting of the American Association for Cancer Research on April 12, 1999. My account is based on an Associated Press report published April 13, 1999.

44   "Mediterranean Diet May Reduce Heart Risk," *Circulation: Journal of the American Heart Association*, February 16, 1999.

45   Source: *Men's Health* magazine.

46   Adapted with permission from Environmental Nutrition, 52 Riverside Drive, Suite 15A, New York, NY 10024.

47   Johns Hopkins University Health Information, April 9, 1999.

48   Source: Group Health Cooperative.

49   Source: Group Health Cooperative.

50   This study was conducted by the University of Washington's Cardiovascular Health Research Unit. Rozenn Lemaitre was the lead author. The report was published in *Archives of Internal Medicine*, April 12, 1999.

Index